MAPPA MUNDI
Hereford's Curious Map

MAPPA MUNDI
Hereford's Curious Map

by

Sarah Arrowsmith

Logaston Press

LOGASTON PRESS
Little Logaston Woonton Almeley
Herefordshire HR3 6QH
logastonpress.co.uk

First published by Logaston Press 2015
Reprinted 2015
Copyright text © Sarah Arrowsmith 2015

All rights reserved. No part of this publication
may be reproduced, stored in a retrieval system,
or transmitted, in any form or by any means,
electronic, mechanical, photocopying, recording
or otherwise, without the prior permission,
in writing, of the publisher

ISBN 978 1 906663 91 9

Typeset by Logaston Press
and printed and bound in Poland by
www.lfbookservices.co.uk

Contents

Acknowledgements

I have many people to thank for their help: my husband Keith for his patience; my daughters Kate, Emma and Jenny and my son Jack for reading the drafts and my father John for also reading the drafts; the Revd Canon Christopher Pullin, Chancellor and Master of the Library of Hereford Cathedral, for his invaluable advice and for the many discussions we have had; Dr Rosemary Firman, Hereford Cathedral Librarian; and Mrs Rosalind Caird, Hereford Cathedral Archivist.

I am also indebted for their encouragement, support, discussions and advice to all the medievalists with an interest in Hereford's *mappa mundi* who I have met at various universities and conferences.

All photographs of Hereford's *mappa mundi* are by permission of the Dean and Chapter of Hereford Cathedral and the Hereford Mappa Mundi Trust; other photographs are individually credited. The image of the whole map reproduced on page *viii* shows the map in its current state and colour. Where details of the map are used as illustrations accompanying the text, the contrast has been improved and the background lightened to a more yellowy/golden colour, so that details can be more clearly made out.

Preface

Hereford's *mappa mundi* has been extensively studied. Scholars have produced comprehensive and informative accounts of the map's sources and legends; experts have studied the handwriting and images to reveal much about the production of the map; and others have researched contexts so that the map can now be more easily understood within the medieval literary, classical, art-historical, cartographic and theological traditions. For students and visitors to the cathedral with an academic interest in the map there are many books summarising current scholarship, setting the map alongside other medieval maps, and pointing the way to further research.

However, there is little yet that tries to bring to life the map's different images and texts and understand how medieval visitors to the map over 700 years ago might have seen or read them. For instance, when medieval viewers of the map looked at the picture of the pelican, or the lion, what legends came into their minds? Or, faced with the image of a creature with its mouth in its belly, what might they have thought? And what was the significance of the Pillars of Hercules? How did viewers of a world map at the beginning of the 14th century understand the cosmos? What did the Red Sea mean to them? In April 2013 I gave a series of four talks to volunteers and staff at Hereford Cathedral aiming to begin to address these and other similar questions. Afterwards a number of people very kindly said that they had enjoyed the talks, and asked me if they could have copies of the notes. So for those who asked, I apologise that it's taken me so long to respond, but here, finally, and in the form of a book, are the notes. I hope they are more easily readable than my original scribbled observations might have been.

Sarah Arrowsmith
December 2014

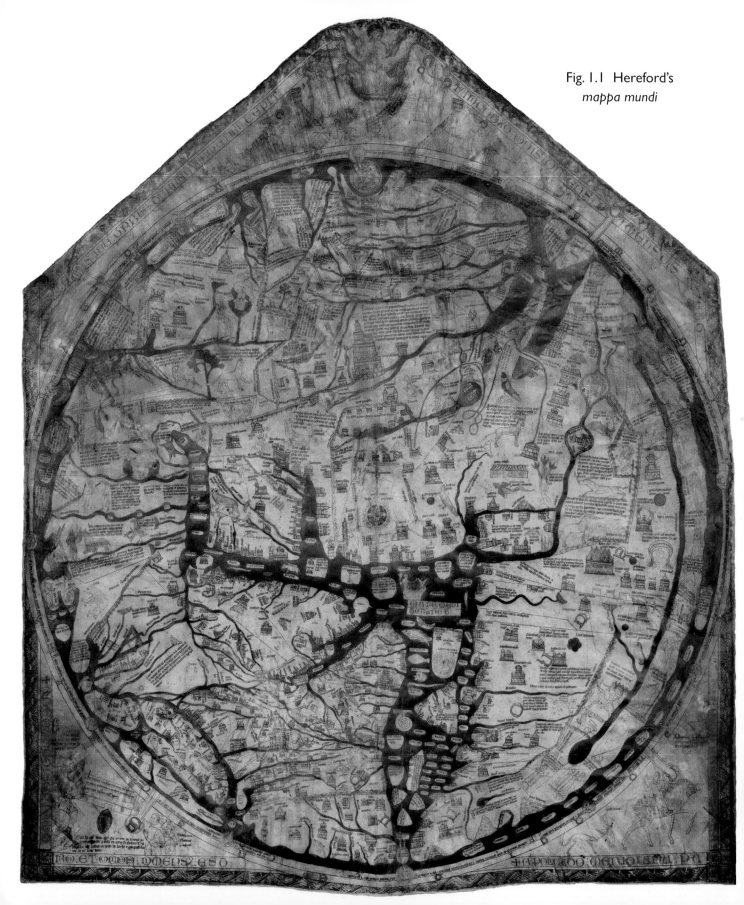

Fig. 1.1 Hereford's *mappa mundi*

1   A Curiosity in the Library

'Amo[n]g other curiosity in this Library are an Map of the World draw[n] on Vellum by a Monk kept in a frame w[i]th two doors – w[i]th guilded and painted Letters and figures.'[1]

Thomas Dingley, 1684

This book is an introduction to Hereford Cathedral's *mappa mundi*. It paints a very broad background to the picture of the curious, by-gone world that is captured by the map's text and images, and its chapters explore different features of that world. In all, it aims to demystify some of the strange and intriguing characteristics of the map, and see them within the context of an age and a world view very different from our own (Fig. 1.1).

Mappa mundi means, in Latin, 'cloth of the world'. Measuring 1.59 metres tall from the base to the apex, and 1.34 metres across at its widest point (5 feet 2 inches by 4 feet 4 inches), Hereford's *mappa mundi* is the largest complete 'cloth of the world' that is known to have survived from the Middle Ages. The whole design is a pentagonal shape, a bit like the gable end of a house, with the world itself shown inside a circle. Three scenes drawn and annotated outside of the circle, in the top and two bottom corners of the pentagonal border, enrich and complete the meanings and messages of the map.

The underlying design within the circle of the Hereford map's world follows a similar layout to a number of other maps of the time, and was probably familiar to the educated, religious community of Hereford Cathedral in the late 13th and early 14th centuries. Yet with Jerusalem in the centre, the earthly paradise at the top, and the Pillars of Hercules at the very bottom of the map, this 'cloth of the world' bears little resemblance to the world map we expect to see today. Moreover, the coastlines are at first unrecognisable, and the world is populated by strange and mythical creatures. A race of people without heads, a basilisk and a unicorn all have a place in this curious world. And here, too, the sites of Biblical stories like Noah's Ark, and classical legends like the Golden Fleece, jostle for position with medieval trading towns and places of pilgrimage. Surrounding the whole, the letters *MORS* spell out 'Death' in Latin: a grim warning that this world of the Middle Ages may be intriguing, exciting and full of wonders, but ultimately it is inescapably precarious.

For the Christians of the time, their destiny after this earthly life was decided at the Last Judgement, and the doomsday drawing at the apex of the map reminds the viewer unequivocally of this fate (Fig. 1.2). Christ reigns above the world, his arms uplifted, displaying the wounds of the crucifixion. He is flanked by angels bearing instruments of the passion: the cross, nails, a sponge and a spear. To his right

Fig. 1.2 The picture of the Last Judgement, or Doom, at the top of the Hereford map

the redeemed rise up from their coffins and enter the gates of heaven, but to his left the damned, chained and stripped of their worldly possessions, are led by a winged demon towards the mouth of hell.

Today, for a society accustomed to the mathematical and scientific accuracy of modern geography, Hereford's *mappa mundi* with its myth, mystique and warning of the inexorable day of doom might seem naïve and unsophisticated in the extreme. In its own time, though, it is likely that the map would have appeared far from unsophisticated. Containing over 1,000 written inscriptions, covered with drawings, and pointing to the destiny of humanity, the *mappa mundi* is like a diagrammatic and pictorial encyclopaedia of the medieval Western Christian world. For its contemporary viewers and readers it must have seemed a stunningly impressive display of knowledge.

The Materials of the Map

The map is drawn onto one large sheet of vellum made from the skin of a single calf, and experts believe that the quality and thickness of the skin suggest that the calf was well nourished and cared for.[2] It is tempting to suggest that perhaps it was suckled and raised in a field near Hereford with the specific purpose of providing the vellum for the map, but as there are no known surviving records referring to the commissioning and production of the map, this has to remain conjecture.

The first stage in making the map was to prepare the calf skin. The skin would have been thoroughly soaked in lime solution, de-haired, washed again, stretched on a frame called a herse, and scraped with a crescent-shaped knife called a *lunellum* to remove all the remaining flesh and hair. Once it was dry, it could be taken off the herse and trimmed to shape. The map is drawn onto the flesh-side of the vellum. Freshly prepared, the vellum would have been a creamy-white colour with a smooth finish, but today, more than seven hundred years after its preparation, the skin is wrinkled and in places shows signs of stress. The vellum has warped considerably from its originally smooth condition, seeming to 'puff outwards, giving an unfortunate effect a bit like a duvet on a bed. These distortions can be seen clearly represented on the three dimensional scan made by Factum Arte in 2013 and now displayed at Hereford Cathedral alongside the map. According to the conservator Christopher Clarkson, much of this distortion is due to repairs to the vellum carried out in the past, which have restricted the natural expansion and contraction of the skin, causing 'banking' and 'bellying'.[3] It takes little imagination to realise that the pentagonal shape of the map faithfully records the shape of the calf's skin. The animal's head would have been at the top, with its legs at the four corners of the frame inside which the map is drawn.

The written texts on the map are still black and clearly defined, suggesting that a good quality ink was used. Most probably the scribe would have made his own ink using oak apple gall, iron sulphate (vitriol), gum arabic and perhaps even wine. And for the illuminations, the artists would probably have mixed pigments like red ochre, yellow ochre, and verdigris with water and egg. The colour blue was sometimes made from lapis lazuli, which would have been particularly precious and expensive, so it was reserved for illustrations depicting the purity of the sacred or divine. On the map, the words of Christ are written in blue. Another and cheaper source of blue, however, was azurite, found in copper ore deposits. Plans to scientifically examine the inks and paints in the near future will help determine what they were made from and may yield interesting insights about the materials used to produce the map.

Fig. 1.3 (left) A detail of the winding stems and leaves that decorate the map's outer border (rotated 50° anticlockwise)
Figure 1.4 (right) Window in the South Choir Aisle in Hereford Cathedral, with naturalistic winding stems forming borders (Photograph by Gordon W. Taylor MBE LRPS)

The Date of the Map

At a conference held at Hereford Cathedral in June 1999, Malcolm Parkes, an expert in the field of manuscripts and early handwriting, presented a paper on the palaeography, or handwriting, of the map. By looking at the style of the letters and the particular ways in which the strokes of the letters were formed, he was able to draw a close comparison with the writing in a manuscript of medical and scientific texts, MS Ashmole 399, held at the Bodleian Library in Oxford. This manuscript is believed to have been written sometime between Easter 1298 and 1299. He concluded that the scribe of the Bodleian manuscript was also the scribe of the map, and that he worked on the map sometime between 1290 and 1310.[4]

At the same conference, Nigel Morgan's paper on the art historical aspects of the map suggested a similar date. Morgan pointed out that the fashion for the particular style of naturalistic winding stems and leaves that decorate the map's outer border (Fig. 1.3) does not appear in England until the end of the 13th century, and that there is a similar pattern in windows in the South Choir Aisle at Hereford Cathedral dated *c*.1300 (Fig. 1.4). He also noted that although such decorative borders are rare in manuscripts there is, interestingly, a similar border in MS Ashmole 399, the manuscript Malcolm Parkes had identified as being written by the scribe of the map. Additionally, Morgan looked at the crucifixion pictured in the centre of the map (Fig. 1.5), noting that similar crucifixion drawings, with a pronounced 's-shaped' hanging curve of the body and uplifted arms 'cannot be paralleled in England until 1280-1290', but in the years between 1280 and 1310, they are numerous. Examples in Herefordshire, dated *c*.1310-1320, can be seen in the stained glass at the Church of St Michael and All Angels at the village of Eaton Bishop (Fig. 1.6).[5]

For some years previous to this conference, it had been generally believed that the date of the map's production was somewhat earlier, but both Parkes' and Morgan's conclusions indicated that the map had been completed sometime between the years 1290 and 1310.

The Making of the Map

In the Middle Ages book manufacture was a process of painstaking copying by hand, and just as books were reproduced in this way, so the design for the map would have been copied from another map or exemplar. Through their analysis of the handwriting and the artwork of the map, Parkes and Morgan were able to construct a picture of how this work was carried out in stages. Once the vellum had been prepared, the circular outlines of the world and the city of Jerusalem were marked onto its surface. Next an artist drafted the coastlines, rivers and mountain ranges with lead plummet, and then the historical places, beasts and peoples, being careful to leave space for the texts. Morgan believes that a second artist took over from here to add the cities, ink over the work already drafted and complete the decorative foliage of the map's border. Newly inked and painted, the blue of the rivers and green of the seas would have been vivid, as would the red of the Red Sea. The vellum itself would have been clean and creamy white, not the time-worn, dirty, yellowish colour it is today. The map was almost certainly vibrant with colour.

After the pictures had been completed, the scribe added the texts. Parkes believes that, given the size of the map and the practicalities involved, the scribe was very unlikely to be copying directly from a sketch or draft of the map, or even from a book. He suggests

Fig. 1.5 (top) The 's-shaped' crucifixion figure on the *Mappa Mundi*
Fig. 1.6 (bottom) One of the 's-shaped' crucifixion figures in the stained glass at Eaton Bishop c.1310-1320. (Photograph by Gordon W. Taylor MBE LRPS)

it is more likely that the scribe would have been working from small pieces of parchment, or *schedulae*, each containing a separate text that he had previously copied from his exemplar in preparation for the work on the map.[6]

Malcolm Parkes also points to the difficulties faced by the scribe, who would, he says, frequently have had to reposition the map in order to copy into vertical, horizontal or even diagonal spaces left by the artists. His attention would have been divided between remembering units of text containing unfamiliar spellings, and fitting them into the required spaces. Clearly the map's scribe was extremely skilled at his craft. After the scribe had finished, all that remained was for a further craftsman, an illuminator or limner, to add the red and gold display lettering of the outer circle and the main geographical areas.

The Sources for the Map

Scholars have not, to date, discovered a map or text that might have provided the exact wording and pattern for the Hereford map's scribe and artists to copy, but many of the place names and labels on the map also appear on other medieval maps, and many of the texts have been identified as bearing similar wording to information contained in a wide-ranging collection of books available at the time. As well as the Bible, some of these influences include the *Natural History* of Pliny the Elder; a book by Gaius Julius Solinus based on Pliny's work and loosely called *A Collection of Memorable Things*; Hugh of St Victor's *Descriptio Mappa Mundi;* Paulus Orosius's *Seven Books of History Against the Pagans*; the *Etymologies* of Bishop Isidore of Seville; a fictional travelogue about the adventures of a man calling himself Aethicus of Ister; and the *Antonine Itinerary*, a list of places in the Roman empire marking the route from Rome to Egypt.[7] Perhaps more closely related to the Hereford map than these sources, however, is a text discovered by Patrick Gautier Dalché. In 2001 Gautier Dalché publicised his discovery of a late 13th-century text, called the *Expositio Mappe Mundi*, which bears a very close relationship to the wording of the Hereford map.[8] The text, which Gautier Dalché found in two separate collections of manuscripts, describes a map of the world that would have looked more like the Hereford map than any other known medieval map existing today. The wording is very similar, some of the phrases are identical, and there are also descriptions of comparable images placed in the same locations as on the Hereford map.

For example the *Expositio* text describing the islands in the north-east reads: 'In the third island is depicted a man with ears to his heels, labelled: the Faneses are cloaked with the skin of their ears.' On the Hereford map, the third island in the ocean, moving eastwards from the Caspian Sea, contains exactly such a picture, and the only difference between the text of the *Expositio* and the equivalent text on the Hereford map is a capital 'F' in the *Expositio* where the Hereford map has 'Ph' (Fig. 3.1). This and other close similarities suggest that the Hereford *mappa mundi* and the *Expositio Mappe Mundi* were copied from a common source.

The Languages of the Map

The language of the map is mostly Latin, but written around the borders of the vellum are five texts in Anglo-Norman, the sort of French that would have been spoken at court and by educated communities of the time. These texts are all speech. At the very top of the vellum, in the apex of the map, two angels speak to those who have arrived at the gates of heaven (Fig. 1.2). One, on the right hand of Christ, invites the redeemed to enter. The other, on his left, condemns the damned to the fires of hell. Central to the scene, the Virgin Mary pleads with her son for the souls of humanity. Below the circle of the world are two further inscriptions in Anglo-Norman. One, on the left, addresses the audience directly, asking for prayers for the map-maker (Fig. 1.7). The other is an enigmatic, two word phrase, *passe avant*, go beyond, which appears to encourage a rider on a horse to pass beyond the rim of the world (Fig. 5.1). Both of these will be considered in more detail at later stages of this book.

The transposition of 'Affrica' and 'Europa'

Across the breadth of Europe, the word *Affrica* is written in large gold display letters and, similarly, the letters of *'Europa'* span Africa. Many scholars regard this as a mistake; some considering it a mistake of enormous proportions. But it is difficult to countenance that in such a costly and exacting project, a mistake on such a scale might have been allowed to remain, and there are other opinions. Bevan and Phillott, in their extensive work on the map in 1873, remarked that the transposition was possibly intended to 'convey the notion occasionally expressed, that Africa was not a separate continent, but a subdivision of Europe.'[9] However another suggestion is that the transposed labels might represent ideas, topical at the time, which used the language of the science of vision and optics to express figuratively the experience of inner spiritual 'vision'.[10] At the time of the map's construction, the work of scholars like Roger Bacon and John Pecham had made new strides in the study of optics, and words like 'reflection' and 'refraction' were used analogously to describe states of spiritual or moral 'seeing' or 'understanding'. In explanation of these ideas, Peter of Limoges, a Franciscan teaching at the University of Paris at the end of the 13th century, wrote a work called *The Moral Treatise on the Eye*. Reflecting on St Paul's letter to the Corinthians, Peter puts forward the notion that in this earthly life we see as if looking in a mirror.[11] Because of our imperfect nature, he reasons, we are not capable of seeing the true glory of God and see only a mere reflection. After the resurrection, however, or at the moment of spiritual perfection, our vision will be direct, not reflected, and we will finally experience or 'see' the true and un-mirrored nature of God.[12] Applying this to the Hereford map, if the transposed labelling is understood in this context, then instead of a mistake, the reversal of the words *Affrica* and *Europa* might be read as intentional; the reversed golden display lettering symbolising the true and un-mirrored vision of spiritual enlightenment. This feature of the map has provoked a lot of recent interest and will bear considerable research.[13]

The Mapmaker

Thomas Dingley's confident assertion in the 1680s that the map was made by a monk, quoted at the beginning of this chapter, is probably not based on any evidence. As we've seen, it was a series of skilled craftsmen who brought the map to life. Even so, there is a name on the map that seems to identify a designer; the man we might call the 'master map-maker'. A verse written in Anglo-Norman in the bottom left-hand corner of the vellum claims that Richard of Holdingham and Sleaford (then known as Haldingham and Lafford) made and designed the map (Fig. 1.7). But this is not as helpful as it might at first seem. Scholars have had difficulty establishing exactly who this Richard might be. There are records of a cleric called Richard of Battle (*de Bello*, in Latin), who was a rector in Kent and who, by 1265, was a canon

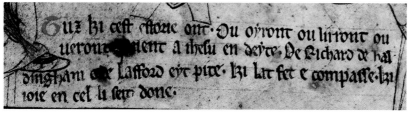

Fig. 1.7 The verse that claims that 'Richard de Haldingham o de Lafford' made and designed the map

of Lincoln Cathedral and appointed to the prebend of Lafford.[14] In the 1270s, this same Richard was treasurer of Lincoln Cathedral, but the Lincoln Residentiary Roll shows that he died in 1278, some time before the date of the map.[15] However there is also mention of another *Richard de la Batayl'* (Richard of Battle) in the household accounts of the Bishop of Hereford for 1289. This second Richard was appointed to the prebend of Norton, became a senior cleric of the Hereford diocese, and died in 1326 after a career that brought him many financial rewards from lands and estates in the Salisbury Diocese as well as Hereford. So we have two Richards. The first could not possibly have been directly responsible for the map because he had died before it was made. The second Richard, however, was very much alive and enjoying the patronage of the bishops of both Hereford and Salisbury during the end of the 13th and beginning of the 14th centuries, and his dates do coincide with the likely date of the map's completion. Even so, there is

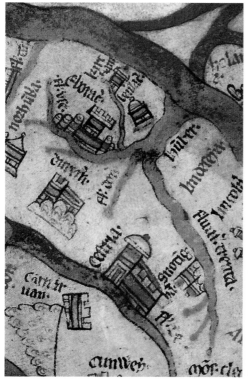

Fig. 1.8 The Ouse-Trent-Humber river system as shown on the *Mappa Mundi*

nothing to indicate that either man is definitely the Richard of Holdingham and Sleaford of the map.[16]

In his analysis of the *Expositio Mappe Mundi,* Patrick Gautier Dalché suggests a family connection between Richard of Holdingham and a branch of the 'de Bello' family known to have established themselves along the banks of the River Ouse in Yorkshire in the 12th and 13th centuries. Gautier Dalché's argument refers to yet another text, one that is bound alongside the *Expositio Mappe Mundi,* and is very likely to share the same author.[17] This text is a description of waterways and coasts. It begins at the city of York and recounts in great detail the banks and sands of the rivers Ouse and Humber, followed by the coasts of Yorkshire and Lincolnshire. Gautier Dalché points out that on the Hereford map, too, the drawing of the Ouse-Trent-Humber river system is peculiarly accurate (Fig. 1.8); an indication that the original source of both the *Expositio* and the Hereford map might have had a connection with the 'de Bello' family of Yorkshire. So although there is no absolute evidence to help identify a map-maker called Richard of Holdingham and Sleaford, Gautier Dalché's work strongly suggests a relationship between the maker of the archetype from which the Hereford map was copied, and the De Bello family who lived in Yorkshire.

The Map's home city

The reference to the Lincolnshire place names of Holdingham and Sleaford has contributed to a belief held by some that the map was made in Lincoln, and the fact that the Bishop of Hereford at the time of the map's construction, Bishop Richard Swinfield, had previously been chancellor of Lincoln Cathedral adds weight to this case. It is not difficult to believe that the map might have been made in Lincoln, not in Hereford, and then brought to Hereford under Swinfield's direction. Moreover, the idea of a Lincolnshire provenance seems to be supported by the importance given to the city of Lincoln on the map (Fig. 1.9). Bevan and Phillott comment on this, and so does Professor Paul Harvey in his book *Mappa Mundi: The Hereford World Map*.[18] The drawing of Lincoln is detailed and large; it appears to be one of the most prominent places in England. The River Witham, the hill, the houses lining the hill, and a building that could be either the cathedral or the castle at the top of the hill, are all clearly distinguishable. But why should Lincoln figure significantly? At the time of the map's production, the diocese of Lincoln was large and important, including places as far south as Oxford, so perhaps it is not surprising that Lincoln is given such prominence. However, a number of scholars favour the idea that the detail in the drawing implies that the map-maker was familiar with Lincoln, suggesting that this evidence of familiarity adds to the number of indications in favour of a Lincolnshire provenance. Moreover there is yet another piece of circumstantial evidence that seems to lend weight to the argument in favour of Lincoln. A list of book borrowers in a 12th-century manuscript in Lincoln Cathedral library contains, amongst the titles of various books, the words *'mappa mundi'*. It seems that someone at Lincoln Cathedral in the 12th century borrowed a *mappa mundi* that was then one of the holdings of Lincoln Cathedral's library. A number of people have linked this entry in the Lincoln borrower's list to the Hereford map, believing it to perhaps refer to the exemplar from which the Hereford map was copied, and holding it as further evidence that the Hereford map began life in Lincoln. The connection between the booklist entry and a map is by no means certain, as in the Middle Ages the term *'mappa mundi'* might equally have referred to a descriptive text, but even so, the evidence for a Lincolnshire provenance seems fairly convincing, if circumstantial.

However in 1989, Martin Bailey, a journalist working for the *Observer*, saw in the British Library a sketch of the map inside a wooden frame. The sketch had been drawn by John Carter in the 18th century (Fig. 1.10). Bailey wondered if the wooden frame pictured

Fig. 1.9 Lincoln is at the top of this extract from the *Mappa Mundi*, drawn in some detail, with Hereford almost worn out, perhaps by being constantly pointed out by visitors to Hereford Cathedral. Worcester is shown just above Hereford, and the Clee Hill is the prominent feature near the centre of the extract.

Fig. 1.10 John Carter's drawing of the *Mappa Mundi* in the 18th century showing the map inside a wooden frame (BL Add. MS 29942)

Fig. 1.11 The backboard found at Hereford Cathedral as a result of Carter's sketch

in the drawing might still exist, so he arranged to visit Hereford Cathedral, meet the Chapter Clerk, and search for it. The men duly met and explored the cathedral out-buildings where, amongst a pile of rubbish in what had been a stable, they found an old, gable-shaped wooden frame that looked very like the frame of the Carter drawing (Fig. 1.11). This is what Martin Bailey said about it:

> … after shifting through considerable debris, we found a large wooden panel leaning against a wall, covered with a thick layer of dust. It had a decorated Gothic gable and on the front was the unmistakable outline of the mappa mundi, picked out in nail holes. It was clearly the central panel depicted in the Carter drawing …[19]

In 2004 a tree-ring analysis of the wood that makes up the frame was undertaken by Ian Tyers, a dendrochronologist from Sheffield University. This analysis showed that the wood came from oak that was felled during the last quarter of the 13th century and the first decade of the 14th century, with the possibility that this date might be narrowed to between 1289 and 1311. This matches very closely the date range suggested by Parkes and Morgan for the construction of the map. Furthermore, the analysis showed that the data collected correlated with data held for tree ring sequences from the western area of England. In his report of the analysis, Ian Tyers names, specifically, Herefordshire, Gloucestershire or Monmouthshire, commenting that: 'This is an unexpected outcome since the Hereford Mappa Mundi has hitherto been thought on documentary and pictorial evidence to have been made in Lincoln and subsequently moved to Hereford.'[20] So it certainly looks as though the wooden back panel for the map was made in or around Hereford. But questions remained: When was the map fixed to the panel? Had the map perhaps been made in Lincoln and fixed to the panel at a later date?

Excitingly, markings and fixing holes on the wooden frame make it look very likely that the map was fixed to the panel when it was drawn. This likelihood is made all the more plausible by a conical hole in the centre of the wooden panel that coincides with the hole in the centre of the map. The conservator responsible for the care of the map, Christopher Clarkson, has suggested that this hole could very well be the compass point for the circular outline of the world.

So, although it is not possible to be totally certain, it now looks fairly likely that, despite suggestions of a Lincolnshire provenance, the map was probably made in Hereford and can legitimately be called the 'Hereford' *mappa mundi*. But this does not exclude the possibility that Hereford's map might have been copied from a lost exemplar, whether text or map, that had connections with Lincoln Cathedral.

A Round or Flat World

Even though the known inhabited part of the world is drawn into a flat circle, this doesn't mean that everyone in the Middle Ages thought the world was flat. Scholars today believe that by the 13th century the sphericity of the Earth was a well-established notion, at least amongst the educated. Probably originating in Ancient Greece, the concept of a spherical Earth had been accepted and adopted by Roman philosophers and early Christian writers. One of those who had written about the Earth as a sphere was the Northumbrian monk Bede (AD 673-735), most famous for his *Ecclesiastical History of the English People*. In another work, *De temporum rationem*, 'The Reckoning of Time', which sets out the Christian calendar and calculates the dates of Easter, Bede says that the Earth is 'not merely circular like a shield or spread out like a wheel, but resembling more a ball, being equally round in all directions'.[21]

Bede's writings were widely copied and circulated over the following centuries, and the spread of his works, and those of other writers who expounded similar theories about the shape of the Earth, makes it very likely that by the time of Hereford's *mappa mundi,* the sphericity of the Earth was more or less common knowledge in educated communities. That's not to say, of course, that there wasn't opposition to this idea, and it is quite likely, also, that the average countryman tilling his strip of land and struggling to grow enough to pay his tithes and feed his family probably never even thought about such things.

But although it was known that the Earth was a sphere, the medieval, Western Christian understanding of the cosmos was quite different from ours. In the Middle Ages, following previous classical models, Christian scholars put the Earth at the centre of the universe. They believed that the Earth was motionless and surrounded by nested crystalline spheres in which the sun, moon, planets and stars all orbited the Earth. Beyond these spheres, the outermost sphere was the 'highest heaven', the 'empyrean'. This was where God sat, enthroned and surrounded by the saints and angels. Viewers of the Hereford map in and around the year 1300 may well have examined it with this medieval cosmological scheme in mind, believing the map to represent a motionless orb at the centre of the cosmos, around which all other celestial bodies revolved, and over which God presided.

The unfamiliar look of the Map

At first sight the landmasses form unfamiliar and inexact shapes, the seas and waterways are all but unrecognisable, and until you realise that east is at the top, it is well nigh impossible to locate individual countries or cities. But all becomes clearer after some of adjustment of expectation. In fact, the landmasses and waterways shown inside the circle of the *mappa mundi* are not actually a picture of the whole world. The circle shows only the known inhabited part of the northern, temperate hemisphere. This was called the ecumene, after the Greek, οἰκουμενη, meaning the inhabited portion of the world.

In modern, cartographical terms, the Hereford map might be likened to an inexact sort of azimuthal projection with Jerusalem at the centre. If you swivelled a globe around until Jerusalem instead of the Arctic Circle faced upwards, directly towards you, with Scandinavia to the left and Africa to the right then, roughly speaking, that is the view of the world pictured on the Hereford map. The orientation is to the east, so that east is at the top, west at the bottom, north to the left and south to the right.

The image on the left below (Fig. 1.12) is, very roughly speaking, the part of the world that is on the Hereford *mappa mundi*. With this in mind, and comparing it to the Hereford map on the right (Fig. 1.13), it becomes easier to see that the British Isles are at the bottom on the left. The seas have become more like rivers and the islands themselves are strangely inflated and disproportionately large, but perhaps this is predictable, given that the map is made in England! Moving round anti-clockwise from the British

Figs. 1.12 and 1.13 The image on the left is, very roughly speaking, the part of the world that is on the Hereford *mappa mundi*. The British Isles are at the bottom on the left, and moving round anti-clockwise, the Strait of Gibraltar is in the centre at the bottom of the circular outline, and the Mediterranean Sea flows upwards and inwards from there. The Red Sea and the Persian Gulf are the 'fingers' of water at the top on the right.

Isles, the Strait of Gibraltar is in the centre at the bottom of the circular outline, with the Mediterranean Sea flowing upwards and inwards from there. The Red Sea and the Persian Gulf are the 'fingers' of water at the top on the right.

As well as depicting the land masses in an orientation and projection unfamiliar to a modern audience, the Hereford map is compressed into an underlying scheme that adhered to an already established tradition of representing the world as a circle divided into three continents by a 'T'. Asia occupies the top half of the circle, while the bottom half is divided by the Mediterranean Sea, with the European countries on the left and Africa on the right. According to the story in Genesis, after the great flood the population of the world was wiped out, and the nations were repopulated by the sons of Noah: Japheth in Europe, Ham in Africa and Shem in Asia. This informs the basic T-O diagram, one that appears many times over in medieval manuscripts (Fig. 1.14). For Western Christians of the time, the T-O symbol conveyed the cross at the centre of the circle of creation.

It is difficult for us to grasp the immensity of the Bible's importance in medieval Christendom. Throughout the Middle Ages, theologians and philosophers aspired to interpret the history and destiny of humanity in terms of the writings of the Bible. Many encyclopaedic chronicles were written to describe and interpret God's creation, all that was in it and the place and destiny of humanity within the divine scheme. Some of these books were illustrated by T-O diagrams or maps. The Hereford *mappa mundi* is like a large, very detailed and naturalistic version of a T-O diagram.

Fig. 1.14 A T-O diagram from Isidore of Seville's *Etymologies*. (© The British Library Board, Royal MS 6 C I, f. 108v)

Although this map of the Middle Ages might appear strange and unfamiliar to us, for its contemporary audience it included an astonishing array of textual and pictorial information about a world that had been made familiar through hearsay, or through the writings and travelogues that circulated at the time. Moreover, in the Western Christian culture of the Middle Ages this sort of map showing the ecumene inside a circle was almost certainly not unusual. Though many of the surviving maps of this sort are in books and a great deal smaller than the Hereford map, their frequency suggests that these sorts of *mappae mundi* were commonplace and would probably have been familiar to the educated.

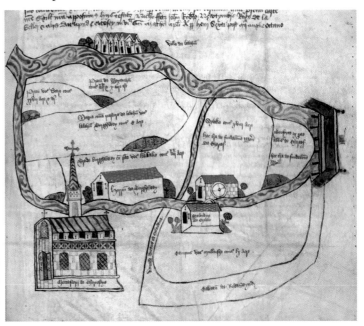

Fig. 1.15 Map of the estate boundaries for Chertsey Abbey. (By kind permission of The National Archives UK).

The Purpose of the Map

Just as today maps are created for many and various reasons (the map of the London Underground, for instance, is vastly different from, say, an Ordnance Survey map), so in the Middle Ages, diverse maps were drawn for many varied purposes. Figure 1.15 shows estate boundaries for Chertsey Abbey, Figure 1.16 is a pilgrimage itinerary drawn by a 12th-century monk called Matthew Paris, and Figure 1.17 is a very detailed navigational chart, probably the oldest of its kind. It shows ports along the Mediterranean and the Atlantic coast lines, and the outline of what looks a bit like a modern map of Italy is just about visible. Figure 1.18 shows a very homely and practical map – the plumbing system of the cathedral church in Canterbury. This is just a sample of the sorts of maps made for different practical purposes by people in the Middle Ages, and each is quite different from the others. What, then, was the particular purpose of Hereford's *mappa mundi*? What did it say to its medieval audience? It obviously wasn't designed to delineate estate borders, or to give a pilgrimage itinerary, and it certainly wasn't a navigational chart.

As we've seen, the circle of the world contains an encyclopaedic collection of geographical, natural, Biblical and mythical images. It is a fusion of classical and Christian learning passed down to the Middle Ages through the writings of classical scholars and early medieval theologians and philosophers, all expressed within a geographical framework dictated by the Bible. Moreover the map also shows the changing weather and seasons. The world is surrounded by twelve winds. Texts around the circumference of the map tell the audience that these winds

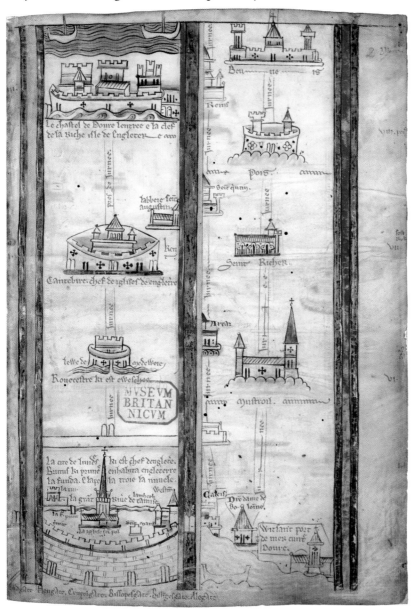

Fig. 1.16 A pilgrimage itinerary from London to Beauvais drawn by Matthew Paris. (© The British Library Board, Royal MS 14 C VII, f. 2r)

Fig. 1.17 The Carte Pisane, a navigational map of the Mediterranean c.1300.
(© Bibliothèque nationale de France)

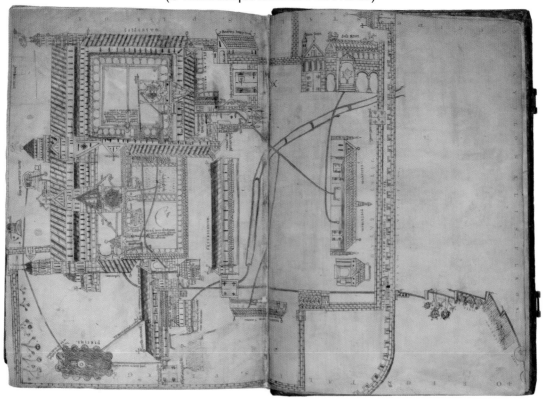

Fig. 1.18 The plumbing system for Canterbury Cathedral
(By kind permission of the masters and fellows of Trinity College Cambridge, MS R 17.1 fols 284v and 285r)

14

can bring warm breezes, kind summers and good harvests, or they can blow icy gales and harsh winters. This is the living world as it was understood by the map's medieval audience. It is a world where history and geography, time and space, destiny and creation, come together under one divine scheme. Perhaps its purpose was simply as an object of devotional contemplation, or perhaps the map was intended as teaching aid. Another possibility is that the map might have been intended as a sort of status symbol to demonstrate the scholarly reputation of the cathedral community in Hereford.[22] There is no totally conclusive evidence about why it was made, where it was housed, or what role it played in the life of Hereford Cathedral, but several accounts do record it being in the cathedral library in the 17th and 18th centuries. In 1684, as we've seen, Thomas Dingley records the map in its triptych in the library, which was then housed in the Lady Chapel. And almost a century later, in 1770 Richard Gough saw the map in the same place. Both Dingley and Gough suggest that the map had once been used as an altarpiece, but there is no further evidence for this being its primary purpose.

Fig. 1.19 The twelve winds on the map are depicted by animal heads with wind streamers coming from their mouths. The wind pictured above blows from approximately east-northeast and is called Vulturnus. The text tells us that it melts and dries out everything, and blows with great power.

More credence is given to the suggestion that the map was commissioned by Bishop Swinfield to play a part in the pilgrimage cult connected to St Thomas Cantilupe. A number of scholars have taken this suggestion further and identified places in the cathedral where the map might possibly have been housed as part of Swinfield's scheme. Daniel Terkla believes it hung in the North Transept beside the Cantilupe shrine, and Thomas de Wesselow would have it in the South Choir Aisle.[23] But whatever the reason for the map's existence in Hereford in the years around the beginning of the 14th century, the map itself had its own narrative to convey. It painted a picture of the world as it was understood by Western Christian thinking of the time, and within this picture it mapped the story of humanity; a story that will be more fully explored in the next chapters.

2 FROM EDEN TO DOOMSDAY: MAPPING THE STORY OF HUMANITY

> And it came to pass that in those days there went out a decree from Caesar Augustus that the whole world should be enrolled.
>
> Luke, 2:1

On the left-hand side of the map, at the bottom of the vellum and below the circle of the world, the seated figure of the Emperor Caesar Augustus hands a sealed document to three men (Fig. 2.1). He wears a papal tiara, indicating that his imperial status is endorsed by the greater authority of God.[1] Above his head is a text from St Luke's Gospel explaining the scene. The words are in Latin but, translated, they read: 'There went out a decree from Caesar Augustus that all the world should be enrolled.' More recent English versions of the Biblical text famously tell how Caesar Augustus decreed that 'all the world' should be 'registered' or 'taxed' as part of the census in Judea under the governorship of Quirinius. This is the reason given for Joseph and Mary's famous journey to Bethlehem, the city of Joseph's ancestors. In the context of the map, though, the decree takes on a slightly different emphasis. Rather than instructing all citizens to register, the map's text implies that Augustus ordered that the world itself should be surveyed and recorded. Accordingly, written on the document he hands to the three men, is the instruction to 'go into all the world and make a report to the senate on all its contents'.[2]

The three men charged with this task are named. They are Nichodoxus, Theodocus and Policlitus. The names and commissions of these surveyors are also recorded in red lettering around the outside edge of the vellum. Here we are told that Nichodoxus measured all the East, Theodocus the North and West, and Policlitus the South. On closer inspection, however, the information offered in the map's border seems confusing because it also tells the viewer that it was Julius Caesar, not Augustus, who initiated the project to map the world.[3] But perhaps this apparent inconsistency might be partially explained. In his study of Greek and Roman maps, classical scholar O.A.W. Dilke makes reference to early sources detailing how in 44 BC Julius Caesar sent out surveyors to embark on an ambitious project to measure the world. The complete project took something like 30 years to complete, by which time Caesar Augustus had become the imperial ruler of the Roman world.[4]

Fig. 2.1 The commissioning scene from the bottom left-hand corner of the Hereford map

The commissioning scene also contains a further important text that relates directly to the making of the Hereford *Mappa Mundi* itself. Placed immediately beneath the seal of Augustus's document is a verse written in Anglo-Norman asking for prayers for the medieval map-maker, who, as we saw in Chapter One, is named as Richard of Holdingham or Sleaford (known as Lafford in the past): *Tuz ki cest estorie ont ou oyront ou lirront ou ueront. Prient a ihesu en deyte. De Richard de haldingham o de lafford eyt pite. Ki lat fet e compasse. Ki ioie en cel li seit done*, 'Let all who have this history – or who shall hear, or read, or see it – pray to Jesus in his divinity to have pity on Richard of Holdingham, or of Sleaford, who made it and laid it out, that joy in heaven may be granted to him.'[5]

The position of the verse in the layout of the whole scene is important. It is placed centrally, beneath the seal of the commissioning document and between the images of Caesar Augustus and the three surveyors. In this arrangement, words and pictures work together to create a visual message; the central placement of the verse firmly links the creation and 'laying out' of the medieval map to a prestigious tradition reaching back centuries, one that looks to both imperial and biblical precedents, claiming the authority not just of Roman antiquity, but also of scripture.

The verse describes the map as an *'estorie'*, an Anglo-Norman word meaning a history, narrative, or story. For medieval viewers of the map, as well as showing the geography of their contemporary world, the map charted the story, or *estorie*, of humanity. It looked to the past, to the birthplace of humanity in the Garden of Eden, and to the future as it was foretold in the apocalyptic prophecies of the Bible. The image of the Day of Judgement spanning the world is compelling and must surely have made that impending and unavoidable doomsday seem very real to the map's contemporary audience (Fig. 1.2). This would be the final reckoning; the dénouement of the story of humanity, and images of damnation and redemption remind the viewer of the judgement that must stand between this world and the heavenly kingdom. The risen Christ sits enthroned with the world at his feet. He raises his hands, displaying wounds of the crucifixion, and behind his raised hands is a banner on which a now indistinct text is written in blue. It reads *Ecce Testimonium meum*, 'Behold my witness', underscoring the meaning of the crucifixion and its imperative for salvation and for the destiny of humanity.

Beneath this prophetic scene, the map's world features important people and events from Christian and Biblical history. Amongst these are Noah's Ark (Fig. 2.4), Abraham (Fig. 2.6) and Moses (Fig. 2.10), men who, in the Bible, marked seminal moments in the establishment of the relationship between God and humanity. St Augustine of Hippo, one of the most influential of early Western Christian

Fig. 2.2 Berwick-upon-Tweed
(rotated 90° clockwise)

thinkers and writers, is also pictured (Fig. 2.18). But the map is not simply a history of the Bible and Christianity. Like most of the Plinian and strange races examined in Chapter Three, for example, many of the entries on the map can be described as non-Biblical or pagan. Sites of antiquity and mythology figure conspicuously. The Pillars of Hercules mark the end of the western landmass (Fig. 2.26), Jason's golden fleece is spread out beside the Black Sea (Fig. 2.22), and Crete, with its labyrinth, occupies a large space in the Mediterranean Sea (Fig. 2.21). Moreover, as well as tales of the past, many cities and towns on the map record their own medieval present. The grandeur of Berwick-upon-Tweed can perhaps be seen as recognition of the ambitions of Edward I (Fig. 2.2), and the elaborate drawing of Paris records its importance in the Western medieval world (Fig. 2.29). Yet the centrality of Jerusalem and the crucifixion (Fig. 2.12 and 1.3), and the over-arching dominance of the doomsday scene, make it clear that on this *mappa mundi*, these contemporary references, along with the many pre-Christian and non-Biblical events, are all players in a universal narrative that is shaped by the Christian God's ultimate plan for all humanity.

The following list describes many of the places, events and people that make up the map's narrative. It is divided into three groups: Mapping Biblical and Early Christian History, Mapping Myths and the Ancient World, and Mapping the World of *c.*1300. The aim has not been to refer to everything included on the map, but rather to choose entries that might have held particular significance for the medieval viewers of the map, and to place them in the context of the world of *c.*1300.

Mapping Biblical and Early Christian History

The Earthly Paradise or Garden of Eden

The book of Genesis, the first book of the Bible, tells how Adam and Eve were expelled from the Garden of Eden because they disobeyed God by eating the forbidden fruit of the tree of knowledge. On the map the Garden of Eden is a circular island in the extreme east, at the top. But although Eden is certainly 'on the map', so to speak, the design of the image is unequivocal in its message that humanity has long since foregone the right to enjoy paradise on earth. Because of Adam and Eve's disobedience, Eden is inaccessible to both man and woman. It is surrounded by a ring of fire and crenelated walls, the gates are firmly shut and the whole garden is separated from the landmasses by water. Inside the gates are the four rivers that were thought to have their source in Paradise – the Nile, Euphrates, Tigris and Indus – and though barely visible now, with the help of modern technology it is just possible to also make out the head of a serpent coiling out of a tree to tempt Eve with an apple. Beneath Eden, on the eastern-

Fig. 2.3 The Garden of Eden

most shore of the world, an angel with a sword sends Adam and Eve on their way. Their shoulders seem burdened, their heads are bowed, and they wring their hands in despair. They are wretched; crushed with the weight of an act of disobedience that will condemn all of humanity to live in a world of sin. In this world there is no return to the Edenic paradise.

The Garden of Eden also holds another particular significance for the narrative, or *estorie,* of the *mappa mundi.* As well as the scene of Adam and Eve's fall, this is the birthplace from which, according to Biblical history, the common ancestry of all races can be traced.

Noah's Ark

Noah's Ark stands high and dry on a long mountain range in the top left hand quarter of the map (Fig. 2.4). The text says, 'Noah's Ark came to rest in the mountains of Armenia'.[6] The drawing of the boat looks something like a model for a child's toy. It has a woven patterned, semi-circular hull, and house-like living quarters complete with a row of five windows and a scallop-edged roof. Through the windows are glimpses

Fig. 2.4 Noah's Ark

of animals, snakes and humans. The story of the great flood is another tale with particular relevance to the map. The Bible tells how God, angered at the corruption of humanity, sent a great flood to cover the Earth. Noah alone was deemed righteous, and God instructed him to build an ark to house his own family and to save specimens of all the living creatures of the Earth. But once the waters had subsided, and importantly for the story of humanity, God made a covenant with Noah that never again would He destroy every living creature. He set a rainbow in the sky as a sign of the pledge, and sent out Shem, Ham and Japheth, Noah's sons, to repopulate the Earth. Japheth went to Europe, Shem to Asia and Ham to Africa, as many medieval T-O diagrams record.

Babylon and the Tower of Babel

Babylon, with the Tower of Babel atop its soaring structure, has a significant and central presence in the eastern, top half of the map (Fig. 2.5).[7] It is pictured as a vast, elaborately decorated architectural construction straddling the River Euphrates. Five storeys high, its dominance seems to state that in its time the Babylonian Empire reigned supreme. The text to the right of the structure is also the longest description on the map. It tells of the founding of Babylon by Nimrod, a descendant of Noah's son Ham, and his wife Semiramis, and gives details of its massive size and construction. This was a city so immense that it could be seen easily from all directions. But Babylon also had a figurative significance. In the last book of the Bible, the Revelation to St John, the city of Babylon embodies images of every kind of evil. In Chapter 18 of Revelation, John sees an angel coming down from heaven and calling:

> Fallen, fallen is Babylon the great! It has become a dwelling place of demons, A haunt of every foul spirit, A haunt of every foul bird, A haunt of every foul and hateful beast. For all the nations have drunk Of the wine and of the wrath of her fornication And kings of the earth have committed fornication with her And the merchants of the earth have grown rich from the power of her luxury.

And in fact, a close look at the map shows the faint image of a demon issuing forth from the walls of the city. On the map, Babylon truly is the 'dwelling place of demons'.

The *turris babel*, 'Tower of Babel', teeters on the city's topmost storey. The legend of the Tower of Babel is in Chapter 11 of Genesis. It tells how the people tried to build a tower so tall that it would reach the heavens, but God punished their arrogance by causing them to speak different languages, and scattering them over the face of the Earth in confusion.

It seems likely that for the medieval audience of the map Babylon spoke of all things sinful, and the Tower of Babel, too, reminded and warned them of the dangers of over-reaching pride and arrogance. Additionally, and importantly for the map's narrative, it also provided a reason for the existence of different languages and races spread across the Earth.

Another much smaller tower, that appears to be labelled *terra babilonie,* 'The Land of Babylon', is pictured further downstream on the banks of the Euphrates. Some scholars argue that it is this tower and not its vast neighbour that represents Babylon itself.

Fig. 2.5 Babylon and the Tower of Babel

Abraham

Fig. 2.6 Abraham

To the right of the long text describing Babylon is an architectural canopy like an aedicule which displays the bust of a bearded man who is not named. However the place name is given as 'Ur', the homeland of Abraham, and the shrine-like structure clearly marks a man of considerable importance, so it is probably safe to assume this is intended as a reference to Abraham. Genesis Chapter 12 relates how Abraham has a specific role to play in God's plan for humanity. Having renounced the Chaldean pantheon of gods in favour of the one, true God, Abraham is chosen by God to leave his home town of Ur of the Chaldees (in modern day Iraq), and travel to a new land. God makes a threefold pledge to Abraham; he will become the father of a great nation, this nation will dwell in a new land, and the people of the nation, Abraham's descendants, will be blessed.

Bethel

Fig. 2.7 Bethel

The city of Bethel is the place where Jacob, grandson of Abraham, dreamed of a ladder between heaven and earth, with angels ascending and descending. On the map, however, Bethel is depicted as a small tower and there is no reference to Jacob's ladder. All the same, for medieval Christians, the place name Bethel would have spoken of Jacob's dream and of that moment of intersection of two worlds; the heavenly and the earthly. The analogy of a ladder or stairway to heaven that could be climbed through prayer or by increasingly virtuous acts was a common notion. One medieval book, called *Scala Perfectionis,* 'The Scale (or Ladder) of Perfection', written by the 14th-century mystic, Walter Hilton, describes degrees of contemplation towards spiritual perfection. Hilton considers how the human soul, in its state of sin, has deviated from God, but how, through stages of contemplative prayer, meditation and reading of scripture, the soul can be reformed in the image of Jesus. The number of manuscript copies of this book still existing today testify to its popularity in the Middle Ages, and evidence of annotations in manuscripts suggest that it was read by clerics and lay people alike.[8]

Fig. 2.8 Lot's wife and Sodom and Gomorrah

Sodom and Gomorrah and Lot's wife

In Chapters 18 and 19 of Genesis, God destroys the cities of Sodom and Gomorrah because of the wickedness of the people. The story tells how one evening two angels arrive at Lot's house in Sodom, a city built on a fertile plain. Lot offers them hospitality, but other inhabitants of the city are hostile. The angels tell Lot to take his wife and children and flee from the city into the hills without looking back. They leave in haste, and as they go God rains fire and brimstone onto the plain and destroys the cities and all their inhabitants. But Lot's wife turns round and is immediately turned to a pillar of salt. On the map, Lot's wife is pictured standing on the east bank of the River Jordan, to the north of the Dead Sea, looking back over her shoulder regretfully at the cities of Sodom and Gomorrah. Today the area north of the Dead Sea is still renowned for salt pillars, so it is easy to imagine that one of these pillars, looking a little like a woman, might have been taken as the salified wife of Lot. Curiously, though, the cities of Sodom and Gomorrah themselves are pictured right in the centre of the Dead Sea. They are drawn as half-submerged tops of towers, with water lapping around their stonework. The medieval map artist was clearly responding to a belief that the cities were engulfed in water, but the account in the Bible makes no reference to this apparent drowning. It would be interesting to know why Sodom and Gomorrah are shown in this way on the map.

Joseph's Storehouses

Some way to the west of the Dead Sea, and in Egypt, is a long low building with a pitched roof and three arched entrances. The label reads *Orrea Joseph,* 'The granaries of Joseph' (Fig. 2.9). This storehouse refers to the story in Genesis about Joseph's rise from his status as a Hebrew servant to become the leader of all Egypt, answerable only to the Pharaoh. In the story, the Pharaoh is troubled by two dreams. One is about seven fat cattle consumed by seven lean cattle, and the other is similar, but about seven

Fig. 2.9 Joseph's granaries

plump grains that are consumed by seven lean grains. Joseph interprets the dreams as a warning of seven years of abundance to be followed by seven years of famine. Grateful for Joseph's warning, the Pharaoh promotes him to govern the land and ensure that provision for the famine to come will be made during the years of plenty.

At the time the map was made, there was a common belief amongst medieval Christians that Joseph's granaries were actually the Pyramids. One medieval book, *The Travels of Sir John Mandeville*, probably written originally in the middle of the 14th century, says that the Pyramids were made to store grain for hard times, stating quite categorically that it's 'not true that the Pyramids are the sepulchres of great lords.'[9] References to pyramids as granaries or storehouses are not found only in manuscripts. An early 13th-century mosaic in one of the cupolas of St Mark's Basilica in Venice clearly shows a pastoral scene with gatherings of wheat being stored inside pyramid-shaped structures. Perhaps the association with agriculture and land management explains why the architectural style of the granaries on the map (and also on some other medieval maps) has a lot in common with English medieval manorial buildings, and seems peculiarly out of place in the Egyptian desert.[10]

The Story of Moses and the Exodus

Moses is pictured on a mountain labelled *Mons Sinay,* 'Mount Sinai'. The mountain lies between two bodies of sea, both painted red, in what should be the Sinai Peninsula (Fig. 2.10). He is bearded and his hands are clasped together in prayer as he kneels to receive the Ten Commandments. Above him the hand of God delivers the tablets of the commandments out of a cloud. Typically for medieval images of Moses after he had received the commandments, he is pictured with golden 'horns'. In the Latin of the Vulgate Bible, the word *cornutam,* meaning 'horned', is used to describe Moses' face as he came down from the mountain after his meeting with God. This was a mistranslation of the Hebrew text, which led to Moses being given actual golden 'horns' in many medieval paintings. [11] Modern English versions of the Bible more accurately use the word 'shining' or 'radiant'.

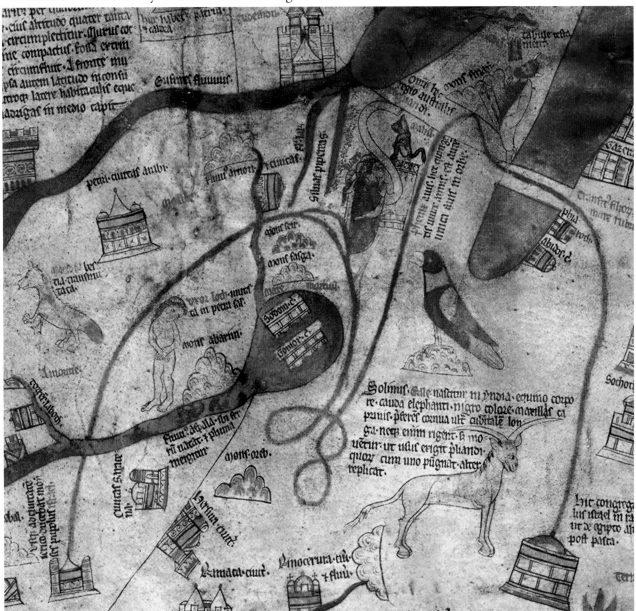

Fig. 2.10 Moses, and the line representing the trail taken by the Children of Israel in their flight from Egypt

There are many other texts and pictures on the map that might have been recognised by the map's medieval audience as playing a part in the story of Moses. In chronological order, the first is a text placed to the right of the Red Sea, by the source of the Nile. This text names the area 'Moyse', that is, 'origin of waters', and perhaps refers to the place where the infant Moses was found by Pharaoh's daughter, apparently abandoned in a basket and floating amongst bulrushes.[12] Chapter 2 of the second book of the Bible, Exodus, says that the Pharaoh's daughter called the child Moses because she 'drew him out of the water'. The toponym 'Madian' or 'Midian' also appears, referring to the place where Moses sought sanctuary after killing an Egyptian slave driver. But apart from the name *Madian* there is no other direct reference on the map to the earlier part of Moses' history. In far more explicit detail, though, is the line that marks the journey of the People of Israel as, led by Moses, they escaped from slavery in Egypt. The path begins at

the city of *Ramesse,* 'Rameses', which is depicted as a domed building surrounded by a city wall. This is where, according to Exodus Chapter 12, over 600,000 men, women and children together with livestock in great numbers set out to escape their Egyptian slave-masters. On the map the path follows a route given in the Bible. It first travels eastwards past the cities of Etham, Suchoth and Migdol where the Israelites made camps, and then, recording the tale of the miraculous parting of the waters, it crosses the Red Sea at Pi-hahiroth. Here, a text written in red reads: 'The passage of the Children of Israel through the Red Sea'.[13] As the route of the path reaches the Sinai Peninsula, it passes the picture of Moses kneeling and then skirts an image of four men who are labelled 'Jews'. Recording medieval stereotyping and prejudice, the most clearly visible of these men is identified by a large, hooked nose, and the Jews are pictured kneeling in worship before an altar on which a small calf-like animal labelled *'Mahun'* is defecating. The scene refers to the story in which Aaron, Moses' brother, encouraged the Israelites to worship a graven image of a golden calf while Moses himself was in the mountains speaking with God. The name *'Mahun',* referring to an idol believed to be worshipped by Muslims, was sometimes used in medieval literature

Fig. 2.11 Detail from Fig. 2.10 showing Israelites worshipping the golden calf

as a non-specific term confusing paganism and Islam. A good example is in Layamon's 12th-century chronicle of the history of Britain, the 'Brut' chronicle, named after the mythical Brutus of Troy. Here, the heathen statues of pre-Christian England are collectively described as *'Mahun'.*[14]

Leaving behind the worship of the golden calf, the line showing the path continues briefly and then ties itself in loops in the wilderness, where the People of Israel were condemned to wander for 40 years because of their grumbling and faithlessness. At a couple of places along the way, the line marking the path is crossed with small hatch marks. These are particularly evident in the wilderness loops and just outside Jericho. Presumably the complete path was once decorated with these marks. Eventually the path unwinds, continues around the Dead Sea area and comes to a rest at Jericho, to the west of the River Jordan, where the text reads, 'As far as the city of Jericho Moses led the People of Israel'.[15] In fact, in the story in the Bible, Moses died before making the final crossing of the River Jordan. It was Joshua who finally led the people into the Promised Land.

The map also includes other images and toponyms that might be related to the story of Moses. Amongst them, Mount Horeb, sometimes considered an alternative name for Mount Sinai, is pictured to the west of the Red Sea, and Mount Abarim, associated with Mount Nebo, from where God allowed Moses to see the Promised Land before he died, is drawn on the east bank of the River Jordan.[16]

For Christian theologians of the Middle Ages, the story of the Exodus of the children of Israel across the Red Sea and out of slavery in Egypt held multiple meanings. As well as a historical account, the story was also symbolic of a spiritual pilgrimage, telling of the possibility of freedom from the slavery and sin of this world, and eventual salvation. This kind of multi-layered interpretation of scripture is famously explained in a 14th-century letter written by Dante Alighieri, author of *The Divine Comedy*, to Cangrande della Scala, his patron:

> If we look at it from the letter alone it means to us the exit of the Children of Israel from Egypt at the time of Moses; if from allegory, it means for us our redemption done by Christ; if from the moral sense, it means to us the conversion of the soul from the struggle and misery of sin to the status of grace; if from the anagogical, it means the leave taking of the blessed soul from the slavery of this corruption to the freedom of eternal glory.[17]

For the map's educated viewers of the Middle Ages who sought to understand the divine messages written into scripture, this kind of multi-layered and allegorical approach would probably have been very familiar.

Jerusalem

Jerusalem, at the centre of the map (Fig. 2.12), would have meant many things to the map's medieval audience. It was the city of King David and the site where Solomon built a great temple; it was

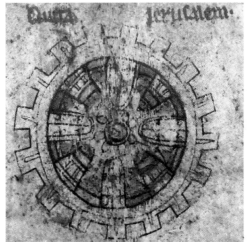

Fig. 2.12 Jerusalem

the place where Jesus lived out his final days on Earth; and it was the city that, as foretold in the prophecies of Revelation, would be re-born at the end of times as a New Jerusalem, freed from the bonds of the sins of humanity. Jerusalem was also a place of both pilgrimage and politics, and it had been furiously fought over during the crusades. There is no attempt at realism in the depiction of Jerusalem on the map. The outline is circular and its external wall is made up of 16 crenelations that enclose four gates facing east, west, north and south with towers between them. In the centre of the city, smaller, inner circles are surrounded by eight rounded shapes, producing a flower-like diagram. According to the Old Testament book of Ezekiel, Chapter 5, verse 5, God says: 'This is Jerusalem; I have set her in the centre of the nations with countries all around her.' Hence, on the map, Jerusalem is at the centre of the world, and in the medieval Earth-centric understanding of the cosmos, this was also the pivotal point around which everything in the heavens revolved. The representation of Jerusalem is undoubtedly symbolic. Moreover, with the cross of Christ's crucifixion seeming to rise up from the circular city, the image created of an orb surmounted by a cross is a powerful statement marking the sacred and spiritual focus of the map's narrative.

Bethlehem

On the map Bethlehem is pictured just below Jerusalem and to the right (Fig. 2.13). The image is an enigmatic depiction of a shrine with its top open standing beneath a canopy. The designation of this shrine is unclear. Bethlehem, however, is well known as the place of Jesus' birth. By the early Middle Ages, a Church of the Nativity had been erected over the top of the cave believed to be the place of Jesus' birth, and it had become one of Christianity's most sacred sites. During the 13th century, though, in 1244, the Khwarazmian Turks conquered Jerusalem and left the Church of the Nativity at Bethlehem devastated. Then in 1263 many of its architectural treasures were removed by the Mamluk Sultan, Baybars. It was not until the early part of the 15th century that repairs were undertaken. So at the time the Hereford map was made, the church at this important and emblematic site had been desecrated and stood in a state of near devastation. Perhaps this is what is signified by the opened casket.

Fig. 2.13 Bethlehem

Mount Tabor

To the left of the image of the crucifixion is a small mountain, set apart, with the River Qishon flowing from it into the River Jordan. The mountain is thought to be the site of Jesus' transfiguration. This was a pivotal moment in the life of Jesus. At the pinnacle of the mountain, three of his disciples, Peter, James and John, witnessed him speaking with Elijah and Moses, and heard the voice of God claim Jesus as his son. Jesus is described as being bathed in radiant light. There is no direct reference to this event on the map, but it is likely that the name of the mountain alone would have held meaning for an audience well versed in the Gospels.

The Journeys of St Paul

Many of the places visited by St Paul on his missionary journeys through Asia Minor, Macedonia and Italy are shown on the map. Amongst them, Antioch, Ephesus, Thessalonica, Corinth, Athens, Malta and Rome are all included, and it is easy to imagine a priest or teacher standing in front of the map and pointing them out to a group of listeners. Their inclusion, however, probably cannot be attributed simply to an intention to plot the journeys of St Paul. These are all places

Fig. 2.14 Mount Tabor and the River Qishon flowing east

Fig. 2.15 Antioch

Fig. 2.16 Patmos
in the Black Sea

that might have been of interest to the medieval audience for multiple reasons. Antioch (Fig. 2.15), as just one example, had been significant to the Roman Empire, conquered by the Rashidun Caliphate and, later, fought over during the crusades. On the map, Antioch is pictured as a fairly imposing city on the eastern side of the River Orontes, to the left of Jerusalem. It has a crenelated city wall and three towers of distinct architectural styles. One is topped with a dome, one has a sort of pitched-roof shaped top with scalloped edges, and the third is like a castle turret. It would be fascinating to know if these three different stylistic features were intended to signify a city that had changed hands between different cultures many times over the centuries.

St John and the Island of Patmos

At the time the map was made, the last book of the Bible concerning the Revelation to St John on the island of Patmos was of great interest to the Western theological thinkers and educated of the day. This book spoke in dream-like, prophetic images of the end of times, the ultimate destruction of the earth, and the emergence of a new Heaven and a new Earth. Many richly illustrated and illuminated manuscripts of this apocalyptic revelation were created. So it is unsurprising to find that the island of Patmos, out of all the many small islands in the Mediterranean and surrounding seas, is one that has been given a named place on the map. Perhaps strangely, though, it has been placed in the Black Sea and not the Aegean Sea. The text on the map simply gives the island's name and no further information.

St Anthony

A line of three buildings in the Egyptian desert, to the right of the upper reaches of the Nile and on the right hand edge of the map, are labelled 'the monasteries of St Anthony in the desert'. The first of these buildings looks very like a European church, but the second and third become increasingly difficult to make out because of damage to the map. St Anthony, sometimes called the Father of Monasticism, was

Fig. 2.17 The monasteries of St Anthony

an abbot and an ascetic who sought solitude in the desert. He was thought to have been often tempted by the devil. One story tells how St Anthony set out on a journey into the desert to find St Paul the Hermit and was confronted by demons in the shape of a centaur and a satyr.[18] The satyr on the map is located just below the monasteries.

St Catherine

The picture of Moses kneeling on Mount Sinai, near the Red Sea, also includes a coffin-shaped feature marked with a cross (Fig. 2.10). There is no text to explain this image, but it seems likely that it represents the shrine of St Catherine of Alexandria. In the Middle Ages St Catherine was revered as a holy virgin. *The Golden Legend*, one of the most popular books of the Late Middle Ages, tells how St Catherine became a bride of Christ and converted many to Christianity through her wisdom and steadfastness.[19] Her refusal to worship pagan idols led the Roman Emperor Maxentius to condemn her to death on a spiked wheel, but the story tells how her faith was so strong that the wheel was miraculously destroyed. Eventually Maxentius had Catherine beheaded, and according to *The Golden Legend* angels bore her martyred body to Mount Sinai, to rest at a place where, centuries later, a church was built and many medieval pilgrims made their way. The spiked wheel was a common instrument of torture that became known as a Catherine Wheel.

St Augustine of Hippo

St Augustine of Hippo is shown standing against a bright red background and framed by the doorway of a decorated church-like building that is topped with three pinnacles (Fig. 2.18). He is clothed in ecclesiastical robes, wears a mitre, and his head is bent forward as he gazes at an indistinct object he is holding in his left hand. St Augustine was one of the most influential of early Western Christian thinkers. He wrote many books of theology. Amongst his theories and philosophies, his ideas about 'Just War' are, even today, often debated in the context of international politics, and his concept of original sin has shaped Western Christian beliefs. The beginning of St Augustine's autobiographical work, *Confessions*, is of particular relevance to the picture on the map. In the first paragraph of the book, Augustine sets out his thesis in words addressed to his creator God: 'You stir man to take pleasure in praising you, because you have made us for yourself, and our heart is restless until it rests in you.'[20]

By the time of the Hereford map, the 'restless heart' had already become a symbol associated with St Augustine, and many medieval images show him holding a heart. This almost certainly explains the picture on the map. Although the small object in the picture is not clear, it is probably safe to assume it is intended to be a heart.

Zozimus

Beneath the monasteries of St Anthony, near the right hand edge of the map, and drawn in an area of, sadly, damaged and age-worn vellum, is a picture of a bearded and hooded figure with bare feet (Fig. 2.19). The drawing is disfigured by time and difficult to make out, but it depicts one of the most recognisably human figures on

Fig. 2.18 St Augustine of Hippo (rotated 90° anticlockwise)

Fig. 2.19 Zozimus (rotated 20° clockwise)

the map. Despite his obvious humanity, though, the drawing of Zozimus completes a line of creatures drawn around the southern rim of the map that represent the Plinian and strange races. Moreover, and intriguingly, he has been placed on a rocky pedestal just like many of these races. According to medieval legend, Zozimus was a priest who encountered St Mary of Egypt in the desert. St Mary had been a prostitute in Jerusalem, but Zozimus recognised her as a true penitent.[21]

Mapping Myths and The Ancient World

Troy

Pictured on the coast of the Mediterranean, to the north of a square-shaped island depicting Cyprus, is a walled city with a tower and three domes rising above its battlements (Fig. 2.20). Hanging over the

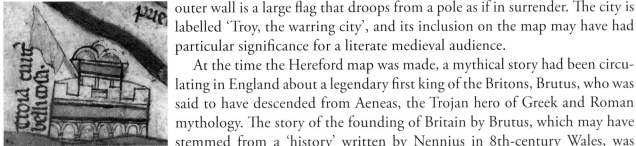

outer wall is a large flag that droops from a pole as if in surrender. The city is labelled 'Troy, the warring city', and its inclusion on the map may have had particular significance for a literate medieval audience.

Fig. 2.20 Troy

At the time the Hereford map was made, a mythical story had been circulating in England about a legendary first king of the Britons, Brutus, who was said to have descended from Aeneas, the Trojan hero of Greek and Roman mythology. The story of the founding of Britain by Brutus, which may have stemmed from a 'history' written by Nennius in 8th-century Wales, was perpetuated in the writings of Geoffrey of Monmouth and also in the works of two poets, Robert Wace and Layamon. Writing in the first half of the 12th century, Geoffrey of Monmouth composed a *History of the Kings of Britain*. This began with the legend telling how, after the fall of Troy, Brutus and his following of Trojans came to the island of 'Albion', which they colonised, and which was renamed 'Britain' after Brutus himself. Wace's poem, *Roman de Brut*, was written in Anglo-Norman in the mid 12th century, and Layamon's poem on the same subject, written in Middle English, is dated sometime around the end of the 12th or beginning of the 13th century.

It is quite possible that many literate medieval viewers of Hereford's *mappa mundi* would have been aware of these 'histories'. For them, the image on the map of Troy's defeat might well have brought to mind notions of a shared ancient heritage between the Britons and the classical civilisations of Greece and Rome.

The Cretan Labyrinth

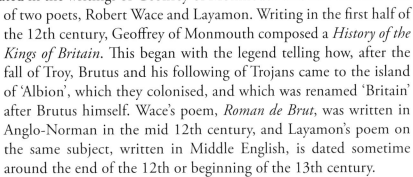

Crete, unmistakeable because of its geometrically defined circular labyrinth, is one of two large islands pictured in the Mediterranean Sea (the other is Sicily) (Fig. 2.21). The text on Crete reads, 'The labyrinth, that is, the house of Daedalus'.[22] In Greek mythology the

Fig. 2.21 The Cretan Labyrinth

labyrinth on Crete was constructed by Daedalus, a master artificer, to house the Minotaur. This creature was half-man and half-bull and had been born of the union between King Minos's wife Pasiphae and a bull. Every nine years the Minotaur demanded the sacrifice of seven young men and seven young maidens. He was finally overcome by the hero Theseus, who attacked him in the centre of the labyrinth and then escaped by laying a thread to help him find his way out. Isidore of Seville describes the Cretan labyrinth as sloping down into darkness and confusion, with 'images of monstrous effigies, and innumerable passages heading every which way'.[23] It is possible that this may have held a figurative meaning for some viewers of the map. There is no drawing of the Minotaur himself on the island of Crete. However, a peculiarly docile looking half-man, half-bull creature does appear to the north of the Hyrcanian forest where the tiger lives. The text here, though, does not apply to the Cretan Minotaur. Instead it refers to the journey of Aethicus Ister, a fictional character in a travelogue from the early Middle Ages, in which he reportedly found 'wild animals similar to the minotaur'.[24]

But the labyrinth may have another significance. At the time the map was made, a number of pavement labyrinths had been built into the floors of cathedrals. Famously, the one built at Chartres Cathedral in Northern France, still exists today. These labyrinths may have represented prayer pathways winding inwards towards a centre that symbolised the central and spiritual focus of pilgrimage.

The Golden Fleece

The fleece of a ram, complete with curling horns and an enigmatic expression on its dead face, is laid out by the northern shore of the Black Sea (Fig. 2.22). The text next to it reads: 'The golden fleece for which Jason was sent by King Pelias'. There are different versions of the mythological story of Jason and the Argonauts, but in essence the story tells how Jason set sail with a band of heroes in a ship named the *Argo*. These Argonauts braved many heroic exploits, encountering both love and treachery, but eventually arrived in Colchis and claimed the golden fleece. The fleece was that of a magical winged ram that had been sacrificed to Poseidon by Phrixus, eventually becoming the constellation Aries.

Fig. 2.22 The Golden Fleece

The Oracles at Delphi and Delos

East of the map's coast of Italy, on the shores of Greece, the head of a bearded man occupies the whole of a peninsula (Fig. 2.23). He faces left, and his mouth is clearly open in speech. The text labels this picture the 'oracle of Apollo', so presumably the head is intended as that of Apollo. The place name is given as Delos, but as Scott Westrem points out, it is more likely that Delphi was meant.[25] In the Ancient world the advice of Apollo was often sought from the priestess, or Sybil, through whom Apollo was believed to speak, and for the ancient Greeks the sacred site of the oracle at Delphi was the centre, or navel, of the world. There was, however, also an oracle on the island of Delos, the birthplace of Apollo. Delos is pictured on the map as a large, nearly circular island to the left of the mermaid. This island is surrounded by a ring of smaller islands intended to be the Cyclades group but, unfortunately, time has rendered the outlines of these surrounding islands a little difficult to make out (Fig. 2.23). The map, following details given by Solinus, Isidore and others, tells us that there are 53 islands in the Cyclades group, and that Delos is situated in the centre.[26]

Fig. 2.23 The oracle at 'Delos' bottom left, the Cyclades top right and the Colossus of Rhodes top centre

33

Parnassus

To the north of Delphi is a range of mountains in an open rectangular shape labelled Parnassus. This was the mountain which was thought to be the home of the muses of poetry and music, and was sacred to Apollo and to Dionysus.

Scylla and Charybdis

In the Mediterranean Sea between Italy and Sicily, either side of what would be the Strait of Messina, are two features looking a little like sea monsters (Fig. 2.24). One, labelled Scylla, is drawn in the shape of an animal head a bit like a dog's, and the creature's mouth is opened very wide to reveal a collection of rounded lumps. The other monster is coiled like a snail's shell, but with a similar collection of rounded lumps at its open end. This creature is labelled Charybdis. The legend of Scylla and Charybdis forms part of the story of Odysseus, who had to navigate between two monsters, one a rock and the other a whirlpool. There are two other similar drawings of a 'Scylla' on the map. One of these, to the north of Scotland, may represent the Corryvreckan whirlpool on the west coast of Scotland, between the islands of Jura and Scarba, but the other lies between the coast of England and France, and Scott Westrem suggests it might be a misunderstanding of the Scilly Isles.[27]

Fig. 2.24 Scylla and Charybdis, with Rome top left

The Colossus at Rhodes

The Colossus at Rhodes was one of the seven wonders of the ancient world. It was a vast statue of Helios or Apollo that stood on top of a column at the entrance to the harbour, but it was destroyed in an earthquake. In popular legend, as in Shakespeare's *Julius Caesar*, the Colossus came to be thought to stand astride the harbour entrance, with ships passing beneath.[28] However, most scholars dispute this, believing that the statue stood on one column only. On the map, the text is written next to a single column on the island of Rhodes (Fig. 2.23). It reads: 'The extremely splendid column'.

Fig. 2.25 The Nile Delta with the Pharos lighthouse and Alexandria on the eastern bank

The Pharos Lighthouse

In the Nile delta, the drawing of a spreading city topped with two tall pointed towers marks the site of Alexandria, founded by Alexander the Great (Fig. 2.25). To the north of the city, joined to the land, is the island of Pharos. Here the fabled lighthouse, another of the seven wonders of the ancient world, is drawn in some detail. In the Middle Ages the Pharos lighthouse was sometimes attributed to Alexander but today scholars suggest it was built by Ptolemy in the 3rd century BC. On the map, the lighthouse has two distinct levels. The first level is a tower topped by a scallop-edged feature with what might be poles for flags standing out at either side. Above this a narrower tower tapers slightly towards the top of the structure, where tongues of red flame show a lighted beacon.

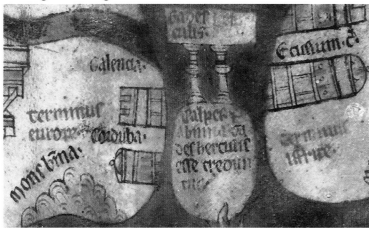

Fig. 2.26 The Pillars of Hercules

The Pillars of Hercules

At the Strait of Gibraltar two columns stand on an island marking the entrance to the Mediterranean Sea (Fig. 2.26). The island appears not to be a real island, but rather a device to support the text explaining the columns. The text reads, 'The rock of Gibraltar and Monte Acho are believed to be the Columns of Hercules'.[29] There are a number of versions of the myth about the

Pillars of Hercules. In one version, Hercules has to travel to the ends of the world where he comes upon a vast mountain which he splits in two, joining the Mediterranean Sea to the Atlantic Ocean and leaving a mountainous column on each side of the narrow entrance to the Mediterranean. In another version of the story, Hercules himself builds the mountains in order to hold up the sky. During the Middle Ages the Columns of Hercules marked what was believed to be the end of the Western world. On the map, a text written in red just inland from the shores of Iberia, and to the left of the columns, reads *Terminus Europe*, 'The end of Europe', and on the opposite side of the columns, in North Africa, a similar text reads, *Terminus Africe*, 'The end of Africa'.

The Alexandrian Story

Alexander the Great (356-323 BC), King of Macedonia, overthrew the Persian Empire led by Darius III and aimed to conquer the whole world. His travels and conquests captured the popular imagination in the 12th and 13th centuries, and many stories about his exploits were in circulation. Reflecting this, the map is unequivocal in its admiration for Alexander. On the border between Africa and Asia, a large elaborate construction is labelled 'Camp of Alexander the Great'. It has ornately patterned walls and five impressive and highly decorated pinnacles (Fig. 2.27). The central and most dominant pinnacle bears a cross, as do the two sides of its lower structure. Considering Alexander the Great pre-dates the birth of Christ by more than 300 years, this is an interesting visual message. On the map, Alexander the Great's

Fig. 2.27 The Camp of Alexander the Great

campaign is clearly seen as part of the Christian mission. Moreover, according to legend, Alexander erected three altars to Athena at each of the furthest points of his conquered kingdom, yet on the map there appears to be no criticism of the pagan designation of his altars. Unlike the altar of the Jews at Mount Sinai, Alexander's altars have no judgemental reference. Three altars of Alexander are drawn in the Far East and two in northern extremes.

But there is yet more detail about Alexander's role as a pseudo-saviour. In the far north and to the east of the Caspian Sea, an illustration clearly shows a wall with four crenelated towers and no gate or opening (Fig. 2.28). This is the wall built by Alexander the Great to protect the world from the pagan nations that inhabit the cold north-east. It blocks the exit and access to a promontory which is also surrounded by mountains on its other three sides. The long text inside the sealed land area describes in detail the unimaginable savagery of the inhabitants. These abominable creatures, we are told, are the sons of Cain who, in a perverse corruption of the Christian sacrament, eat human flesh and drink blood. Another text written

Fig. 2.28 The wall built by Alexander to protect the world from the pagan nations of the north-east

on the opposite side of the wall spells out the threat posed to humanity by these heathens. At the time of the Antichrist, it reads, they will 'burst forth and inflict persecution on the whole world'.[30]

Related to these two texts is a third, written on the island of Terraconta in the Northern Ocean. It says: 'The island of Terraconta, which the Turks inhabit, of the lineage of Gog and Magog, a barbarous and filthy people who eat the flesh of youths and miscarried foetuses'.[31]

All of these texts refer in part to passages in the books of Ezekiel and Revelation, where it is prophesied that at the end of times the evil forces of Gog and Magog will rise up against Israel. But as well as this, and more directly than the Biblical references, the texts also reflect the popular beliefs and histories that circulated in the Middle Ages. The following passage from a work dealing with the end of times, known as the Apocalypse of Pseudo Methodius, describes the same, terrifying event:

Then the gates of the North will be unbarred and out will come the powers of the nations which Alexander enclosed within, and the whole earth will be struck by their appearance and men will become terrified and flee, and, fleeing in terror, they will hide themselves in the mountains and in the caves and among the tombs. And they will be deadened with fear and many will be wasted with terror …[32]

The passage continues to describe horrific and cannibalistic deeds very similar to those referred to on the map.

According to the narrative of the map, then, Alexander the Great is presented not as a Greek war leader, but instead, and in keeping with popular literature of the time, as a heroic saviour of the Christian world.

Mapping the World of *c.*1300

Hereford
During the latter part of the 13th century and beginning of the 14th century, Richard Swinfield, Bishop of Hereford 1282-1317, was engaged in a campaign to promote the pilgrimage cult of his predecessor Thomas Cantilupe. A new shrine had been erected in the recently built and fashionably French influenced North Transept of Hereford Cathedral, and an elaborate scheme of building was embarked upon to direct the flow of pilgrims around the cathedral. As part of this scheme, and probably in order to demonstrate an impressive heritage, a series of effigies of past bishops were designed to line the walls of aisles, and new windows were built to lighten the way.[33] Today most of these windows are of clear glass, but in the 19th century a number of pieces of 14th-century glass were found carefully packaged up and stored away. Some of these pieces were re-installed and it is this 14th-century glass that Nigel Morgan has identified as bearing a similarity with the decorative border of the map.

The map is considered by many to have played an important part in Swinfield's campaign to promote Hereford Cathedral as a place of learning, heritage and, importantly, pilgrimage. However it is often noted that Hereford's own presence on the map is surprisingly unimpressive, and particularly so considering the circumstances in which the map might have been commissioned (Figs. 1.9 and 2.29). The picture of Hereford is small, faded and almost rubbed out. The city symbols representing close neighbours Gloucester, Worcester and Shrewsbury are not particularly imposing themselves, but all are far more striking than Hereford's. The reason for this has been debated by scholars, with some believing that the illustration and place name for Hereford had been added after the map had been completed. However, more recent scholarship suggests otherwise. In his examination of the handwriting, Malcolm Parkes concluded that the entries on the map for Hereford and the River Wye are certainly corrections, but that they were made by the same scribe who wrote the map's other inscriptions, and probably at about the same time.[34] An explanation might be that perhaps Hereford was not pictured on the exemplar that the scribe and the artist were copying from, which would have simply recorded the River Severn, so this would have been what was initially copied. It is easy to speculate that the instruction to add Hereford in order to customise the map for those who had commissioned it, came just too late. The newly inscribed map would need to be altered! Malcolm Parkes suggests that the uncharacteristic roughness of the vellum around Hereford on the map testifies to the scribe's scraping away of the words 'River Severn' in order to make room for the important entry that gave Hereford a place in the world.[35] I have a compelling picture in my head of the scribe, all those centuries ago, penknife in hand, complaining quietly to himself as he carefully scraped off some of the precisely placed original lettering to make room for the words 'Hereford' and 'River Wye'!

Other places of note in the British Isles
The map was made during the reign of Edward I and, as a number of scholars have pointed out, the inclusion of the Welsh castles of Caernarfon and Conwy on the map might be in recognition of his Welsh campaigns. Berwick-upon-Tweed also features. It is very grand, and according to the map's representation of its towers and extensive buildings, it was certainly thought of as a large and prestigious place,

more imposing than almost all other cities and towns in the British Isles (see also Fig. 2.2). Perhaps this is a reflection of Edward I's ambitions in Scotland and the north of England. Further south, the detailed representation of Lincoln on the map has already been mentioned in Chapter 1, but by comparison, the small picture representing Canterbury poses questions. As an archbishopric and the site of the shrine of St Thomas Becket, Canterbury might expect to figure significantly. Instead, it jostles for position with Rochester, squashed into a land area between the River Medway and the River Stour. Perhaps it is an accident of its location, but in size the picture for Canterbury is no bigger than that for Rochester. Looking a little closer at the architectural drawings, though, it is apparent that there is a difference. The icon for Canterbury has ramparts that perhaps suggest a city wall, and it is in fact slightly more complex than Rochester's single building. Perhaps this is an indication of some use of symbolism in the icons representing cities. By comparison with Canterbury's unimpressive icon, though, the picture of York, the second archbishopric, is far more extensive and detailed. A row of buildings spreads along the side of the

Fig. 2.29 The British Isles

River Ouse, and a large tower with an imposing crenelated battlement rises between them. York's prestigious history reached back to its foundation as a Roman capital in the 1st century AD. Winchester, too, as befitting a city of political importance and a site where kings had been crowned, has a fairly detailed picture not dissimilar to York's, though smaller; a row of houses clusters along the River Itchen, with a large structure rising between them. But, unsurprisingly, London, centre of administration, politics and trade, is the most elaborate of all the cities depicted in the British Isles. Pictured on the River Thames, London is shown as a collection of buildings and towers, including one that appears to be flying a flag, gathered around a large and complex structure with yet more towers and pinnacles. Further upstream, a much smaller architectural device locates Oxford, home to one of Europe's oldest universities and alma mater to many key scholars of the Middle Ages.

A particular curiosity of the representation of the geography of the British Isles is Clee Hill (see also Fig. 1.9). Looming large over the Welsh Marches, it covers the whole border between England and Wales and seems, incorrectly, to be the source of both the River Dee and the River Severn: surely an indication that whether the map was made in Hereford or not, the artist was not entirely clear about local geography!

In Ireland the largest city depicted is Armagh, the city of St Patrick. In the early Middle Ages Armagh was home to an important centre of learning.[36]

Rome

Rome figures on the map as a particularly grand architectural structure (Fig. 2.24). It is the largest in Europe except for Paris. Rome held immense significance for medieval Western Christian theologians, and this was not simply because of its history and antiquity. For them, it also embodied the fulfilment of prophecy. Rome was the figurehead of the last of a succession of empires foretold in the Book of Daniel, an empire which, above all, had a mission to overturn pagan nations and evangelise the whole world. It was on this interpretation of history that Paulus Orosius had based his *Historiae Adversus Paganos*, 'History Against the Pagans', written in the early 5th century AD and referred to in the margin of the map.[37] Moreover, centuries later, the Kingdom of Germany and the territories of central Europe became known collectively as The Holy Roman Empire. Successive leaders of this vast coalition of territories adopted the title 'Emperor', and sought coronation from the Pope. The text on the map reads: 'Rome, head of the world, holds the bridle of the spherical earth'.

Paris

The complex of buildings drawn to depict Paris is actually larger than that for Rome, but less detailed (Fig. 2.30). Paris was home to Europe's most important schools of theology and one of the very first universities. Many, if not most of the great theological thinkers of the age had studied and taught in Paris; among them Thomas Aquinas, St

Fig. 2.30 Paris

Bonaventure and Albertus Magnus. Others had also travelled to Paris to study where the great thinkers had gone before. One of these was Thomas Cantilupe, Bishop of Hereford 1274-1282, whose pilgrimage cult Bishop Swinfield later sought to promote. Paris was also the site of Notre Dame Cathedral and the Sainte-Chapelle, built by Louis IX to house his collection of passion relics that included the crown of thorns.

Sadly, the area on the map depicting France, including Paris, has been vandalised by a series of deliberately and randomly drawn lines. Apparently anti-French feelings ran high in Hereford at some point in the map's history.

Pilgrimage to Santiago de Compostela

In the Middle Ages the shrine of the apostle St James at Compostela became an important pilgrimage site. St James was believed to have preached the gospel in the Iberian Peninsula, but having returned to the Holy Land after a dream vision of the Virgin Mary, he was beheaded by King Herod. According to legend his body was then claimed by angels and taken back to Iberia in a miraculous, rudderless boat.[38] The map shows a shrine with a bell-tower complete with a large bell, labelled 'the shrine of St James' (Fig. 2.31).

Pilgrimage in the Middle Ages was a dangerous business, with pilgrims having to negotiate inhospitable landscapes, foreign customs and even warring factions. The guidance of previous travellers would have been hugely important, even more so than today, and there is evidence that books were written with the intention of fulfilling exactly that purpose. A very detailed 12th-century guide book is still kept in the cathedral of Santiago de Compostela. This forms part of the illuminated manuscript known as the *Codex Calixtinus*, sometimes called The Book of St James. Along with liturgy, music and details of miracles, the manuscript gives extensive travel information for pilgrims, including the route to take, the costs involved, local dialects, details about where the best wines, meat and fish are to be found, and even advice that Tiermas in Spain has hot springs – as it still does today!

Some of the places referred to in the *Codex Calixtinus* are also included on the map, but although it is not possible to trace the complete pilgrimage itinerary, research by G.R. Crone during the 1960s shows how a number of the map's toponyms do mark out significant parts of the route. His paper for the Woolhope Club in 1967 observes:

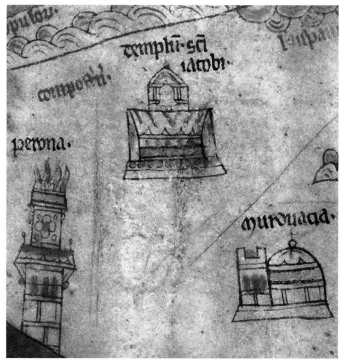

Fig. 2.31 The shrine of 'St Jacobi'
or St James at Compostela

41

In the region of the Pyrenees, we notice the comparatively small and little-known town of Jaca (on the map, Yake) which can only be there as marking the southern end of the Somport pass, a much frequented pilgrim route; to the west are the towns of Pamplona and Astorga, also on this route. An alternative way across the Pyrenees from Dax is shown. North of this point, the route from Paris is recorded in some detail.[39]

It's pleasing to imagine a medieval pilgrim returning to the cathedral community in Hereford after travelling abroad. Peering closely at the map he might search it for places he'd travelled through, and then point them out to his stay-at-home audience, telling tales of adventures and experiences in foreign climes and maybe, at times, enlivening them a little with exaggeration or fantasy.

Trade routes

In his paper of 1965, G.R. Crone points out the inclusion on the map of places in France that were significant for the wool trade to Italy.[40] Where the River Dordogne meets the Garonne and becomes the Gironde is the port of Bourg, and further along the Dordogne are the towns of Fronsac and Libourne. These names all occur in a 14th-century guide to trading written by a Florentine banker and merchant, Francesco Pegolotti.[41] They mark stations along the route that would have been taken by English wool traders heading for the markets of northern Italy. Talking of other routes, Crone picks out a tall mountain with the word *Recordanorum* written along its left-hand slope. He makes the case that instead of being the name of the mountain, this toponym marks an important route for both pilgrims and traders. He says:

> This is undoubtedly connected with the 'Voie Régordane', an important route to the south of France via Clermont Ferrand, the upper valley of the Allier, and the gorges of the Cevennes, Le Puy, Allais and Nimes. Clermont Ferrand (Avernis) is included among the town names, and the mountain is either the Cevennes or the Puy de Dome… This Voie Regordane was important for pilgrimage, and also for trade, being part of an important medieval system from the Mediterranean to the fairs of Champagne.[42]

Crone also identifies place names on the map that pick out parts of an east-west trade route in Germany from Koln to the River Elbe.

According to Crone's research, as well as recording Biblical information and marking sites of antiquity, the map showed geographical information that would probably have been of particular interest to contemporary medieval traders and pilgrims.

In summary of this chapter, the map's narrative is certainly shaped by contemporary theological thinking but, as Crone has shown, this does not mean that the geography of the map is secondary. On this cloth of the world, past, present, destiny and geography, or in other words time and space, are merged into one homogeneous narrative.

3   A Tall Tale: Mr Pliny and his Monsters

'And of the Cannibals that each other eat,
The Anthropophagi, and men whose heads
Do grow beneath their shoulders. This to hear
Would Desdemona seriously incline.'
                    Othello, Act I Scene iii, ll 143-146

There are monsters and weird creatures in the far-off exotic places of the Hereford map. The remote edges of the inhabited world's circumference are peopled with peculiar humanoids whose outlandish departures from our own expectations of human physical and cultural norms appear strange and often shocking. There is a race of people with four eyes and a king with only one eye; a tribe with no mouth who drink through straws, and a tribe with one enormous lip; and there are those whose customs seem to us perverted in the extreme: one race eats the flesh of their dead parents, and another drinks from the skulls of their slaughtered enemies.

Through the window of the map, the medieval world that confronts us appears to be inhabited by the abnormal and abominable. With such images of the Middle Ages, it is no wonder that today the word 'medieval' often becomes a euphemism for 'barbaric', 'uncivilised' or 'ignorant'. Yet these fantastic creatures from another world and another time still hold a peculiar fascination. Moreover, for today's visitors to the cathedral, viewing the map from the security of a modern world made thoroughly accessible through travel and technology, there is a comfortable reassurance that these drawings of weird distortions of humanity belong solely to the world of the Middle Ages. Perhaps our understanding of what it means to be human and living in the 21st century is somehow affirmed through comparison with these strange, alternative images.

But where did these legends about races of not-quite-humans come from, and what did those first viewers of the map think of them?

The notion of strange peoples in the remote parts of the world is not peculiar to the Hereford map. Many other descriptions and images of physically or morally abnormal races occur in manuscript texts, other maps, illustrations and carvings that have survived from the Middle Ages. Strange as these peoples are to us, they were probably familiar to the map's medieval viewers. The literate, book-owning communities of the time of the map's construction would probably have read about them, and those outside of the educated, reading communities may have seen carved representations in the stones and timbers of churches, cathedrals, abbeys and manors. Groups of people are also likely to have gathered around story-tellers to hear and exchange tales of travel, adventure and strange peoples.

A tradition of written accounts of curious peoples inhabiting the exotic, far-away places of the world can be traced to Classical Greece. In the 5th century BC, Ctesias of Cnidus wrote about peoples and cultures in a faraway land loosely called 'India'. And in the 4th century BC, another Greek, Megasthenes, wrote a similar 'history'. It is accounts such as these that the Roman writer Pliny the Elder (AD 23-79) drew on for his encyclopaedic work *Naturalis Historia*, 'Natural History', written in the 1st century AD. Book 7 of Pliny's *Natural History* includes many of the races shown on the Hereford map, and it is because of their inclusion in Pliny's work that they are sometimes referred to as the 'Plinian Races'. Around two hundred years later, and drawing heavily on Pliny for his material, another Roman writer, Gaius Julius Solinus (fl. *c*. AD 200), compiled a work called *Collectanea Rerum Memorabilium*, 'A Collection of Memorable Things'. This was an eclectic assortment of information and myth about the places and peoples of the world, and it became a standard text throughout the Middle Ages. Solinus held the fascination of audiences for centuries, so much so that a printed translation of his work was published in English in the 1580s, some 1,200 years after it was originally written.[1]

Throughout the centuries that make up the Middle Ages, Christian scholars tried to draw together the collected knowledge of humanity within the compass of Christian and Biblical history. Many extensive, encyclopaedic works were written. One of the most significant of these writers was Bishop Isidore of Seville (*c.*560-636 AD). His all-encompassing work on the origins of meanings, called *Etymologiae*, 'Etymologies', is of particular relevance to many of the texts on the Hereford map. Chapter XI of the *Etymologies* deals with the 'portents' or 'unnatural beings' that Isidore sees as signs or omens sent from God. For Isidore, just as there are deformities at birth in individual nations, so the monstrous races can be explained as a deformity within the whole of mankind. Just as Isidore had looked to earlier Greek and Roman writers for many of his sources about the strangeness of peoples in distant parts of the world so, in turn, his own writings became a source of information for subsequent medieval writers. Amongst these were the compilers of some of the bestiaries, which include strange races amongst their beasts.

Another medieval theologian and scholar that should be mentioned is St Augustine of Hippo (354-430 AD). Augustine is one amongst only a few historical people to feature on the map. Throughout the Middle Ages his writings were some of the most frequently acquired theological texts in cathedral and monastic libraries. Amongst the collection still housed in Hereford Cathedral's Chained Library today, 21 of the 227 medieval manuscript books contain his work – a measure of his popularity and influence. Augustine, too, lists these strange races; they appear in Chapter 16 of *De Civitate Dei*, 'City of God'. But Augustine's interest is not primarily in geography, ethnography or etymology, but in theological debate. Did these creatures really exist? And if so, could they be called 'human'? Were they descended from Adam? For Augustine, as for a number of other Western Christian thinkers, the monstrous races posed problematic questions. In *City of God* his final words on the problem are inconclusive: 'The accounts of some of these races may be completely worthless,' he says, 'but if such peoples exist, then either they are not human; or, if human, they are descended from Adam.'[2]

As well as their inclusion in more scholarly, theological writings, the strange races appeared in legends of the amazing travels and exploits of Alexander the Great. In one manuscript of a letter supposedly from Alexander to Aristotle, the author begins by swearing the truth of these marvels as if anticipating a disbelieving audience: 'I would not have believed the words of any man that so many marvellous things could be so before I saw them myself with my own eyes.'[3] The letter continues to relate how Alexander and his troops were attacked by a great multitude of dog-headed people, a fictional race similar to the Cynocephales of the Hereford map. Manuscripts of travellers' tales such as this, like the works of Augustine, Isidore of Seville and Solinus, still exist today in enough numbers to suggest that they were widely available in the Middle Ages.

In addition to this varied range of accounts and discussions, the strange races also figure on a number of other *mappae mundi* that were made around the same time as the Hereford map. This group includes a small world map in a 13th-century book of psalms in the British Library, known as the Psalter world map; a fragment of a world map housed in the Duchy of Cornwall office in London; and the Ebstorf map. Sadly, the Ebstorf map, which was far larger than the Hereford map, measuring about 3.6 metres (12 feet) square, was destroyed in a bombing raid over Hanover in 1943. Fortunately, photographic evidence of the map existed and facsimiles have been created.

These world maps, like the Hereford map, are oriented with east at the top, and clearly show a line of monstrous races on the right-hand side, along the southern rim of the world.[4]

But *mappae mundi* like these are not the culmination of the transmission of legends about exotic races, rather, they play their own part in perpetuating that tradition. Beyond the date of the production of the Hereford map, tales of the explorations of a fictitious knight, Sir John Mandeville, began to be widely circulated amongst reading and story-telling communities, and as in the legends surrounding Alexander the Great, Sir John Mandeville was reported to have encountered monsters and strange humanoid races. Like Shakespeare's Desdemona, captivated by Othello's tales of encounters with 'men whose heads/Do grow beneath their shoulders,' audiences spanning centuries were fascinated by the weirdness and other-ness of these strange, almost human peoples.

Some writers derived moral messages from the deformities of the monstrous races, writing material that was used by preachers in sermons and homilies. One such text, in which the physical deformities of Giants, Dog-heads and other strange creatures become a vehicle for moral instruction, is contained in MS Douce 88, housed in the Bodleian Library in Oxford.[5] According to the text of this manuscript, the extraordinarily large ears of the Panotti people, for instance, are created that way in order to listen to evil. Another moralising work that looks for blueprints of human behaviour in the deformities of Pliny's monstrous races is the *Gesta Romanorum*. Meaning literally, 'Deeds of the Romans', this is primarily a collection of tales and anecdotes with a moral outcome. Scholars believe it was compiled sometime around the end of the 13th century and beginning of the 14th century, and many of the tales reappear in the works of later writers like Chaucer and Shakespeare. It includes the story of 'Three Caskets', for example, which was used by Shakespeare in *The Merchant of Venice*. Amongst the tales of the *Gesta Romanorum*, Chapter 175 is devoted to Pliny's 'wonderful races of men on earth'. The writer lists and describes 16 Plinian Races, assigning to each a moral purpose within God's divine plan. These moral tales perhaps point to a way in which the Plinian Races were viewed by some of the thinkers of the Middle Ages. Their existence or otherwise was not the main issue; what mattered was the way in which their outward appearance might reveal their inner moral status.

Thus the details of the strange races on the map took authority from a tradition of writers participating in a transmission of tales that combined hearsay and fact and that spanned centuries. And however sceptical they might have been, for the Hereford map's contemporary viewers, the re-statement of the words of learned men of the past would most probably have affirmed the validity of the map as an authoritative purveyor of knowledge. No matter how many travellers, merchants and pilgrims might explore the world and return having *not* experienced evidence of monstrous races, the influence of antique writings prevailed, and they took their place on the map. Perhaps fuelled by the fascination of the 'other', tales of creatures that challenged notions of what it meant to be human, both physically and morally, continued to circulate, and Hereford's *mappa mundi* played its own part in perpetuating the tradition.

On the Hereford map the 'monstrous' races populate, broadly speaking, three different areas: the Far East, including the region loosely named India by many of the map's sources; the southern rim of the inhabited landmass, which extends across Africa and into Asia, and which includes races from a fabled 'Ethiopia'; and the North, which incorporates the ancient region of 'Scythia', stretching northwards and eastwards from the northern coast of the Black Sea. In the majority of cases, the peoples of each of these three areas can be loosely categorised into three distinct types. With a couple of notable exceptions (the giants-come-dog-heads and the *monocoli*), many of those on the mainland in the east are fairly normal in appearance, and a number of those pictured wear clothes. The races in the south, however, have peculiar physical deformities, and most of them are represented posing on a pedestal of rocky boulders and facing forwards like curious statues or specimens. A number of scholars have commented on the association in medieval culture between rocky, mountainous terrain and deviance from civilisation, and these races are certainly deviant in their physical appearance. Almost all the races pictured in this southern region are unclothed, another measure of their departure from human norms. In the northern regions, in 'Scythia', most of the races are characterised by moral depravity. There are few drawings, but those there are depict fierce combat or savage cannibalism. The people here are clothed, but although they are human in appearance, they are corrupt in nature. In Scythia, too, there are long and horrific descriptions of menacing, vile races that remain un-visualised and un-drawn on the map; the integrity of the Christian world is constantly threatened by their shadowy, unimaginable evil encroaching from the North.

Beginning in the east, at the top of the map, and moving more-or-less clockwise around its perimeter, the strange races are listed below.

Phanesians, *Phanesii*

The strange figure of a naked, tonsured man cloaked in his own very large ears occupies an island off the north-east coast of the land mass (Fig. 3.1). The text above his head follows exactly the same wording as the *Expositio Mappe Mundi* and tells us that 'the Phanesians are cloaked with their outer ears'.

Fig. 3.1 Phanesians
(rotated 45° anticlockwise)

46

Fig. 3.2 Hippopodes
(rotated 60°
anticlockwise)

Hippopodes, *Ipopodes*

Slightly further east than the island of the Phanesians lies the island where the Hippopodes live. The drawing on the island shows a man with horses' hooves for feet (Fig. 3.2). Hooved Hippopodes are also mentioned by Solinus and Isidore.

Chinese, *Seres*

Next to an elaborately drawn city symbol with a tower and pinnacle rising behind a city wall is a text saying that the *Seres* are the first people to live beyond the desert, and that they trade in silk. The city is labelled '*Samarcan civitas*' (Fig. 3.3). Scott Westrem suggests that because of the association with the silk trade, this city might represent Samarkand, an important trading post on the silk road. Geographically speaking, however, Samarkand should be located not in eastern, but in central Asia.

Fig. 3.3 Samarkand

Fig. 3.4 People of the Ganges

People of the Ganges, *Gangines*

The map tells us that 'according to Solinus, the Gangines live beside the Ganges'. In the drawing, two fully clothed humans are scrumping apples from a tree that grows in the mountains (Fig. 3.4). One is knocking them off with a stick, while the other picks them up. But he is not eating the apples. He is sniffing them. The explanation is written the other side of the River Ganges and below the mountains of the Hindu Kush, where the legend reads: 'According to Solinus: those who dwell near the source of the Ganges live solely from the scent of wild apples; if they smell an offensive odour, they die instantly.'[6] The *Expositio Mappe Mundi* also refers to Solinus' account.

Pandeans, a people of India, *Pandea, gens Yndie*

South-east of the Gangines live the Pandeans. The Pandeans have no king; instead they are ruled over by a woman. This female governance, unusual for the Middle Ages, is marked on the map by a drawing of a warlike woman wearing a helmet and carrying a spear (Fig. 3.5). She is fully clothed. The text on the map is identical to the text in the *Expositio Mappe Mundi* and follows the words of Solinus, saying simply, 'Pandea, a people of India ruled by women'.[7]

Fig. 3.5 Pandeans

Pygmies, *Pigmei*

Not far from the Gangines and Pandeans are the Mountains of Gold, watched over by dragons and perhaps, with a little imagination, glowing in the eastern sun. West of these mountains are the mountains of India, where the Pygmies live. The drawing is of four miniature but warlike human figures lined up across a rocky landscape (Fig. 3.6). They wear helmets and carry shields. The map closely follows Isidore of Seville's text, telling us that 'pygmies are humans one cubit high'.[8]

Fig. 3.6 Pygmies

Fig. 3.7 Giants

Giants, *Gigantes*

Two sexually engrossed 'giants' with dog's heads and tails are drawn below Paradise, next to the scene of Adam and Eve's expulsion. Tales of Alexander the Great relate how he met giants in India, but the obvious promiscuous intent of these 'giants-come-dog-heads', and their placement on the map so close to the scene of expulsion, suggests a reference to the descent of angels in the Book of Enoch.[9] This lapsed group of angels were said to have sworn an oath and 'bound one another with curses' in order to descend to earth and take wives of the 'fair and beautiful' daughters of men. They taught their human wives charms and spells, and the wives 'became pregnant and bore large giants'.

Gautier Dalché observes that the *Expositio Mappe Mundi* does not include reference to an actual drawing of dog-heads, but that '*Cynocephales*' are mentioned in the text as being 'above' the altars of Alexander. This is exactly the place where the Hereford map's dog-headed 'giants' are drawn, and Gautier Dalché suggests that this is an indication that the map described by the *Expositio* had a similar picture in a similar place.[10]

The association between Dog-Heads, or Cynocephales, and Giants is common throughout the Middle Ages. St Christopher, who was purported to be a Giant, was sometimes represented with a dog's head. There are two incidents of Cynocephales on the map; the other is in Scythia, on the northern edge of the landmasses.

Monocules, *Monoculi*

In this drawing, a peculiar one-legged creature is lying on his back, sheltering from the sun beneath a large, nine-toed foot (Fig. 3.8). The text on the map tells us that he can move extremely swiftly with his one leg. Monocules, usually called Sciopods (Shady-feet), are a recurring feature of medieval culture, appearing in architectural decoration and drawings at the margins of books, as well in travel writings, chronicles and maps.[11] There are two of them on the Hereford map, one in 'India' and one in 'Africa'. For the medieval viewers of the map these two Sciopods, although one is labelled *Monoculi* and the other *Scinopodes* (Fig. 3.9), would probably have been instantly visually recognisable.

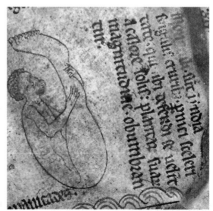

Fig. 3.8 Monocules

Corcina people, *Gens Corcina*

Some distance south of the Pandeans, beyond the sacred mountain of Jove, live the Corcina people. There is no drawing, but the text tells us that in their land, shadows fall northwards in winter and southwards in summer.

Satyrs, *Satirii*

A tall humanoid figure with hooked beak, animal ears and horns fills a large space south of the eastern end of a second 'Nile' river that runs parallel to the southern rim of the map's landmass (Fig. 3.10). He has cloven hooves and carries a staff. Unfortunately the text describing him is almost completely indistinct. The only readable word remaining is '*Satirii*'. The drawing follows Isidore's description in all but size. Isidore's text reads: 'the Satyrs are little people with hooked noses; they have horns on their foreheads and feet like goats'.[12]

Fig. 3.9 Sciopods (rotated 10° clockwise)

Fig. 3.10 Satyrs (rotated 25° clockwise)

Fig. 3.11 Fauns

Fauns, *Fauni*

Westwards from the Satyr, and in the region of the Upper Nile, is a Faun (Fig. 3.11). Greek legends associate Fauns with the god Pan, who traditionally has the hindquarters of a goat, but the creature on the map is half horse and half man. Bearded and wearing a crown, he carries a serpent held in his left hand. Isidore talks of Satyrs and Fauns in the same sentence, but this creature is clearly very different from the map's Satyr.

Fig. 3.12 Ambari (rotated 30° clockwise)

Ambari, *Ambari*

The picture of the Ambari on the map is very indistinct, but a figure holding a long staff can just about be made out (Fig. 3.12). He points in one direction, while his feet turn the opposite way. The legend on the map reads: 'A people

Fig. 3.13 Amyctyrae
(rotated 30° clockwise)

without ears, called Ambari, the soles of whose feet are opposed'.[13] Westrem points out that this is a mixture from two separate sources. Solinus describes the 'Psambari' as living in a region where no animals, not even elephants, have ears, and Isidore talks of the 'Antipodes', 'who have the soles of their feet twisted behind their legs'.[14]

Amyctyrae, *Gens labro prominenti*

On the northern banks of the Nile a naked figure reclines backwards on a rocky crag in what must surely be a very uncomfortable position (Fig. 3.13). A very strange growth comes out from his upper lip and extends over his head, shielding his face, and he points upwards. Just above him the sun, labelled *'sol'*, throws out flames of heat. The text on the map gives him no title, reading simply, 'people with a protruding lip'.[15] But despite the lack of a label, a literate medieval audience would probably have recognised him as an Amyctyra. A race called the Amyctyrae are mentioned by a number of authors including Isidore, and they also feature in the Douce Bestiary, where the author's moral take on them is that 'the mischief of their lips will cover them'.[16]

Sciopods, *Scinopodes*

In this image the Sciopod is standing on his one leg, leaning on a long, sturdy walking pole (Fig. 3.9). (See also the entry for *Monoculi*.)

Fig. 3.15 Hermaphrodites

People with fixed mouth, or 'Straw drinkers', *Gens Ore Concreto*

Pliny, Solinus and Isidore all mention a race of people in the east with monstrous faces, whose mouths are sealed and who feed through a hollow straw. John Block Friedman suggests that this legend might have its origins in the Greek abhorrence of the barbarians' love of beer, which they drank through a layer of barley grains, using a straw to suck up the liquid.[17]

Fig. 3.14 'Straw drinkers'

Hermaphrodites, *Gens uterque sexus*

The picture on the map shows a bearded and turbaned figure raising his/her left arm as though waving (Fig. 3.15). He/she has one female breast on the right-hand side, and both male and female genitalia. The map tells us that Hermaphrodites are 'either sex' and 'unnatural', but makes no mention of Isidore's claim that they 'sire and bear children in turn'.[18]

Himantopods, *Himantopodes*

South of the River Nile and east of the Philli are the Himantopods. Their name implies that their feet are strapped together (Friedman calls them 'Strap-feet').[19] They are pictured crawling on all fours and wearing a military helmet crowned with a long dangerous-looking spike (Fig. 3.16). Although Solinus mentions the Himantopes, he makes no reference to curious headgear.

Philli, *Philli*

Pliny tells of a mountain on the Ethiopian coast that glows with eternal fire and, perhaps with this in mind, the map's designer locates the Philli near the 'burning mountain', *mons ardens*. The picture on the map is of a mother clasping her hands in despair as her infant child is overcome by snakes, and the text reads: 'The Philli test the chastity of their wives by exposing their new-borns to serpents.' (Fig. 3.16)[20] Horrific though this sounds, Solinus, following Pliny, explains that the Philli (though both Solinus and Pliny call them 'Psylls', after a King Psyllus) had developed immunity to snake bites, and that they safeguarded the future of their race by allowing the babies to be bitten. This sounds like a form of immunisation, but the text points more to a moral than a medical issue. In this 'trial of poison', as Solinus calls it, if the babies did not survive, the father was assumed to be not of the Philli and the distraught mother was accused of adultery.[21]

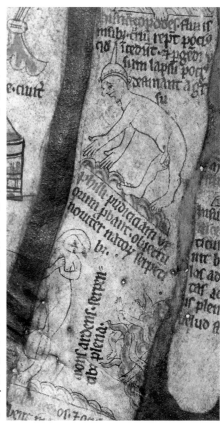

Fig. 3.16 Himantopods (top) and Philli (bottom)

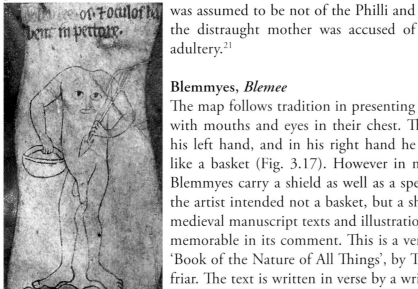

Fig. 3.17 Blemmyes (rotated 20° anticlockwise)

Blemmyes, *Blemee*

The map follows tradition in presenting the Blemmyes as headless creatures, with mouths and eyes in their chest. The map's Blemmye holds a spear in his left hand, and in his right hand he carries an object that looks a little like a basket (Fig. 3.17). However in many other manuscript illustrations Blemmyes carry a shield as well as a spear, so perhaps it is more likely that the artist intended not a basket, but a shield. Blemmyes occur frequently in medieval manuscript texts and illustrations, but one particular manuscript is memorable in its comment. This is a version of the *Liber de Natura Rerum*, 'Book of the Nature of All Things', by Thomas de Cantimpré, a Dominican friar. The text is written in verse by a writer known as the Clerk of Enghien, who includes his own moral comment. He compares the physical disfigurement of the Blemmye to moral depravity, and then goes on to say,

Fig. 3.18 Epiphagi
(rotated 30°
anticlockwise)

Fig. 3.20 Marmini
Ethiopians (rotated
40° anticlockwise)

…Are there any people like this in our own land? Yes, and you need not search further for them. What are they? Why they are lawyers … who have their mouths in their bellies…[22]

Perhaps the people of the Middle Ages were not so very different from ourselves!

Epiphagi

On the map a nameless female figure with no head, but with eyes across her shoulders, gazes directly at the viewer. (Fig. 3.18) She holds a walking pole in one hand and in the other brandishes what is perhaps a club. Isidore mentions 'other neckless' people, as well as Blemmyes, but he doesn't name them. However, Pliny names a race with eyes in their shoulders the *Epiphagi*.[23]

Troglodytes (Cave-dwellers), *Trocoditee*

The map tells us that Troglodytes 'are very swift, they live in caves, eat snakes and catch wild animals by dancing or jumping on them'.[24] The illustration is of three male troglodytes with rather ugly faces peering out from the openings of their separate caves. One of them is eating a snake. Jagged mountain peaks rise above the caves, and below, a naked and bearded man grasps a gazelle-like creature by the horns. Presumably he is a Troglodyte who has caught a wild animal by dancing on him.

Fig. 3.19 Troglodytes
(rotated 30° anticlockwise)

Marmini Ethiopians, *Marmini Ethiopes*

Solinus's account of the Marmini says they are men who live on the coast of Ethiopia and can see as well as if they have four eyes. On the map, this tribute to their keen eyesight is depicted literally; the Marmini has four eyes (Fig. 3.20). According to the *Gesta Romanorum*, the four-eyed Marmini signify a righteous people who fix their gaze, figuratively speaking, in four directions. They look to God, who they fear; the world, from which they desire freedom; the devil, whom they reject; and the flesh, which they chastise. The member of the Marmini on the map carries and points to a T-shaped staff. Perhaps this is a tau-staff, a form of crozier with a T-shaped cross at its head. If so, his gesture might signify an intention to live virtuously, as suggested in the *Gesta Romanorum*.

Gangine Ethiopians, *Gangines Ethiopes*

On the African coast, opposite the Canary Islands, two bearded people stand facing each other (Fig. 3.21). They are clothed only in hats and hold long walking poles. Who they are is a bit of a mystery. The map tells us they are the Ethiopian Gangines, in whom 'there is no friendship', but gives us no more information. This race does not appear to have anything in common with the Gangines of 'India', and is not mentioned by Solinus or Isidore.

Agriophagi Ethiopians, *Agriophagi Ethiopes*

According to the map, which follows Solinus, the Agriophagi Ethiopians eat only the meat of leopards and lions, and have a Cyclops-like king with one eye in the middle of his forehead (Fig. 3.22).

Races named but not drawn

Four races are named as living on the opposite banks of the Nile to the Philli; these are Barbarians, Gaetuli, Natabres and Garamantes. Each of these titles is written in red, suggesting, as Westrem points out, that the map's maker(s) probably believed the title 'Barbarian' referred to 'a separate ethnicity'.[25]

Fig. 3.21 Gangine Ethiopians (rotated 45° anticlockwise)

Fig. 3.22 Agriophagi Ethiopians (rotated 50° anticlockwise)

It is in the northern regions of the map that we find the longest and most horrific descriptions of savage peoples, and here, also, the map sometimes offers moral judgement. The first creature we come across, however, is neither monstrous nor barbaric. Working clockwise, these races are:

Gansmir

A figure on skis is drawn at the far edge of Scandinavia (Fig. 3.23). He wears what many people have described as a 'bobble hat' and seems to be carrying a ski-pole. However his pole is topped by a 'T', and is perhaps intended as a Tau crozier. Perhaps, too, his 'bobble hat' is actually a bishop's mitre? However, the text next to him is unclear and unhelpful, and scholars to date have offered no conclusive explanations. This is another image on the map that will bear a lot more research.

Cynocephales (Dog-Heads), *Cynocephales*

In this drawing the two Dog-Heads sit facing each other (Fig. 3.24). Unlike the Cynocephales in 'India', these two do not seem preoccupied with sex. Their mouths

Fig. 3.23 Gansmir

Fig. 3.24 Cynocephales (left) and Griste (centre)

are open and their heads tilted slightly back as though in animated conversation. They each wield an axe with one hand, but with the other they point, a gesture that in medieval art often signifies speech. There is nothing in the written text on the map to indicate what their conversation might be about, but perhaps a clue is to be found in the Douce Bestiary, where the barking voices of the Cynocephales are said to signify 'detractors and fomenters of discord'.[26] It is easy to imagine that these two Cynocephales on the map are hatching a mutinous plan. The writer of the *Gesta Romanorum* also takes a moral, though slightly different, stance. Here, Cynocephales represent preachers who 'ought to be clad in animal skins, that is, in bitter penance for their untruths and vices, and held up as an example to everyday folk'.[27]

Griste, *Griste*

The Griste are placed to the south of the Cynocephales, on the banks of a mysterious River Corvuus that flows into the Black Sea (Fig. 3.24). Westrem points out that this river does not appear in any of the map's known sources or analogues. A man wearing a tall pointed hat is shown leading a horse draped with what appears to be a flattened human figure. The text tells us that the Griste are extremely wicked; they make clothes for themselves and their horses from the skins of their enemies.

The Lineage of Gog and Magog, *Gog et Magog*

The map tells us how the island of Terraconta is inhabited by '… the lineage of Gog and Magog, a barbarous and filthy people who eat the flesh of youths and miscarried foetuses'.[28] In The Revelation to St John (Chapter 20: 7-10), Gog and Magog represent the enemies of God, roused in an evil alliance with Satan and poised for the final onslaught on the Christian world:

When the thousand years are over, Satan will be released from his prison and will go out to deceive the nations at the four corners of the earth, Gog and Magog, and to gather them for battle; they are as numerous as the sands of the sea. They marched up over the breadth of the earth and surrounded the camp of the saints and the beloved city.

On the map there are no drawings of Gog and Magog. Imagination is left to conjure the evil and barbaric for itself, and there is somehow something far more menacing in the unshaped substance of pure evil, than in a clearly delineated drawing.

The Catharum of Scythia, *Catharum Sithe*
A text written north of the shores of the Black Sea between two rivers, the Silis and the Meotides, repeats words of Solinus, and tells of the Catharum. Unlike other races in the north, the Catharum are not morally corrupt. These are a unique people who have condemned the use of gold and silver and saved themselves from public avarice. There is no picture.

The Scitotauri of Scythia, *Scitotauri Sithe*
The Scitotauri live north of the Catharum. Again repeating the words of Solinus, both the Hereford map and the *Expositio Mappe Mundi* tell us that the Scitotauri of Scythia kill strangers for sacrifices.

The People of the Scythians, *Scitharum gens*

Fig. 3.25 Scythians

Further north still, two armed figures are drawn in full combat (Fig. 3.25). Both are helmeted and carry a shield. One fights with a large knife, the other with a mace. The text next to them lists their characteristics: they live in caves, love fighting, make drinking cups from the skulls of their enemies, and drink the blood straight from the wounds of those they have killed. The map's moral judgement is that they are 'loathsome'.

The Essedones of Scythia, *Essedones Sithe*
There is no picture of the Essedones, but their customs are listed in detail. On the death of their parents they gather a group of friends together to sing funeral songs, and then eat the meat of their dead parents, believing this to be better than leaving it for the worms.

Fig. 3.26 Anthropophagi

Anthropophagi

Alongside the block of text about the Essedones is a picture of two cannibals wielding large knives and tucking into a feast of blood-spewing human limbs (Fig. 3.26). One wears a pointed hat, and the other wears a double-pointed hat not unlike a jester's cap. The closest text on the map is that describing the Essedones, but Scott Westrem believes these cannibals represent the Anthropophagi. He refers to the *Expositio Mappe Mundi*, which places a description of cannibals in this area and names them *Antropofagi*.[29] Gautier Dalché observes that this, like the description of the drawing of the Phanesians with very large ears, is one of the few *Expositio* entries that refer to an actual drawing.[30]

Hyperboreans, *Yperborei*

There is no picture of this race. The description is written inside a rounded peninsula in the north that is surrounded by coastal mountains. It follows closely the words of Solinus and the text of the *Expositio Mappe Mundi*. Far from being corrupt, the Hyperboreans are a 'most blessed', *beatissima*, race. They live in peace, and 'when they are tired of living, they throw themselves off a famous cliff, believing this to be the best form of burial'.[31]

The Arimaspi, *Carimaspi*

To the south of the peninsula where the Hyperboreans live is a drawing of a winged griffin confronted by a group of attacking warriors (Fig. 3.27). One of the warriors clearly has only one eye. According to the text on the map, the Arimaspi fight with griffins for emeralds. There is no mention of them having only one eye, but Solinus and the *Expositio Mappe Mundi* both refer to the Arimaspi as being 'one-eyed', *monocoli*. On the map the Arimaspi are called Carimaspi. Scott Westrem suggests that the additional initial 'C' is due to a scribal misreading of the exemplar.[32]

| Fig. 3.27 Arimaspi | Fig. 3.28 Albanians |

Albanians, *Albani*

A small naked man with a large penis holds a walking staff with one hand and points to his eyes with the other (Fig. 3.28). The text on the map, which follows Solinus, says that the Albanians 'have grey eyes and see more at night'.[33]

The inhabitants of Capharica

In an island off the north-eastern coast of the mainland, a text tells of forests, and inhabitants who have many weapons and who are skilful in destroying cities.

The Stork People, *Cicone gentes*

Here the map gives simply a name, but the drawing is of a stork-like creature with arms, holding a walking staff (Fig. 3.29). The *Gesta Romanorum* speaks of beautiful men with the head, back and neck of a crane. For the writer of the *Gesta* they represent judges 'who ought to have long necks in the manner of cranes in order to think wisely on the heart first, before they offer sentence of the mouth …'.[34]

The Accursed Sons of Cain, *fili Caim maledicti*

In a perverted mockery of the Eucharistic sacrament, the map tells us that the 'accursed' sons of Cain 'eat human flesh and drink blood'. There is no drawing of the sons of Cain, but a wall fortified by four imposing turrets stretches across a wide isthmus on the Caspian Sea. The text, which is one of the longest on the map, relates how an earthquake caused the mountains to

Fig. 3.29 The Stork People

tumble and surround the land, and tells how Alexander the Great built an indestructible restraining wall. The large peninsula beyond the wall is surrounded by mountains. At the foot of the wall, to its south side, is a further text referring to Solinus and likening the sons of Cain to the Anthropophagi and Essedones. The *Expositio Mappe Mundi* has two very similar entries.[35] For medieval viewers of the map, these entries would have held particular significance. The Book of Ezekiel in the Bible, like the Revelation to St John, prophesies the final battle of the end of times, when a mighty horde of the forces of evil will invade from the remotest north and arouse the wrath of God. On the map, the might of this northern army is held back by Alexander the Great's fortifications. (See also Chapter 2, pages 36-37.)

Other races
A number of other races are named but not drawn, and very little other information is given about them. Amongst these are the Huns of Scythia, *Huni Sithe*, the Hungarians, *Hungri*, and the Slavs, *Sclavi*.

These, then, are the weird and monstrous races that inhabit the edges of the medieval world that is the Hereford *mappa mundi*. Although it certainly stretched the credulity of some thinkers of the Middle Ages to accept the physical existence of these creatures, they were nevertheless displayed on the map. These exotic peoples maintained a presence at the extremes of the world's circumference, as if on the edges of knowledge, and although their existence might be ascribed to myth, their deviant physical and social characteristics were often seen allegorically, in a figurative or moral way, as embodying truths about God's divine plan for the nature of humanity.

4 MYTH AND REALITY:
WHERE THE UNICORN MEETS THE RHINOCEROS

But ask the animals and they will teach you;
The birds of the air and they will tell you;
Ask the plants of the earth and they will teach you;
And the fish of the sea will declare to you.
Who among all these does not know that the hand of the Lord has done this?
New Revised Standard Version of the Bible, Job, 12: 7-8

The animal kingdom held a particular fascination for the artists and craftsmen of the Middle Ages. They recreated a world of prowling, flying and slithering creatures that populated the margins of manuscript pages, entwined their tails and necks around the ascenders and descenders of letters, or peered out through the foliage of architectural carvings. Real beasts and fantastical creatures alike were chiselled into the stonework of churches and cathedrals, carved into woodwork, and skilfully drawn into the intricate decorations of hand-crafted books. The animal kingdom pervaded the nooks and corners of medieval life. So it is not surprising to find that the Hereford *Mappa Mundi* is covered with pictures of animals. Some are zoologically recognisable but many others are from the world of myth, legend and hearsay. Whether real or invented, though, for medieval viewers of the map the beasts of the world held a particular significance that stemmed from an interpretation of the natural world that was very different from our own. The thinkers of the Middle Ages were not concerned with biological and scientific questions in the way we are today. Their enquiry began not with 'how?' or 'why?' but with theological questions. They saw the stamp of God on all of creation and they believed that God's moral lessons for mankind were written into the behaviours of the animal kingdom. Their study of zoology, therefore, was concerned with unravelling and understanding what they believed to be divine messages embodied in the habits and behaviours of the beasts of the world. Ants, for example, modelled shrewd and cooperative industry, while elephants were monogamous, showing loyalty and faithfulness. Moreover, medieval thinkers believed that God's didactic intention was expressed not just through an animal's embodiment of moral characteristics, but also in its figurative representation of scripture. Just as Christ died and rose again after three days, so it was that the lion, by his roaring, awoke his cubs into life three days after their birth. The pelican's behaviour, too, was thought to embody the meaning of the resurrection. In the same way that Christ shed his own blood for the sake of humanity, so also the pelican was believed to draw blood from its breast to revive its dead young. For the people of the Middle Ages the natural world was like a book in which God's purpose for sinful humanity might be read; and many books of beasts (bestiaries) were written, to interpret that world and point the way to redemption.

Yet the animals included in the bestiaries were often fanciful, bearing only a slim relationship with zoological reality. Many of the characteristics of these beasts had originated in fascinating stories and travellers' tales about exotic creatures that had been handed on by authors from Greek and Roman civilisations. The compelling fascination of these tales was enduring. Storytellers over the centuries re-told and re-fashioned the tales for their own audiences, exaggerating and inventing encounters with the beasts of foreign lands, until some of these had morphed into unreality, and mythological creatures came to be included in accounts of the natural world. These stories lent themselves particularly well to the allegorising bent of the Western Christian writers and thinkers of the 12th and 13th centuries.

Putting aside the flights of fancy of storytellers over the centuries, the main shaper of the moralities of bestiaries was a text called the *Physiologus*. This was essentially a book of Christian ethics taught through animal behaviours. It was originally written in Greek, possibly in Alexandria. The date is disputed, with some scholars believing it was made around the 2nd century AD and others dating it as late as the early 5th century AD. Translations exist in many languages including Latin, Provencal, Armenian, German, Old English and Old Icelandic; the many translations being proof of its extensive popularity.[1] An Old English verse version of the *Physiologus* survives today in Exeter Cathedral. This version was written in the 9th or 10th century, several hundreds of years after the book was first conceived, and is attributed by some scholars to Cynewulf.[2]

The text of the *Physiologus* contains descriptions of animals followed by an allegorical, Christian interpretation of their habits. In the Exeter Cathedral manuscript, the panther, for example, is described as 'kind, attractive and friendly', just as 'The Lord God, giver of Joy is gracious to all creatures'. On the other hand the whale is not trustworthy. When the whale is hungry he opens wide his jaws and with enticing odours lures unwary fish into his mouth until it is full, 'then, in one instant, he snaps his fierce jaws together about the swarming prey'. The moral to be learned is spelled out:

> Thus it is with anyone who, in this fleeting time, full oft neglects to take heed to his life, and allows himself to be enticed by sweet fragrance, a lying lure, so that he becomes hostile to the King of Glory by reason of his sins.[3]

The text continues to describe how for these heedless people, the doors of hell will be thrown wide – a dire warning for all those looking for a life of easy luxury!

Over the centuries after its creation, medieval writers copied and re-used material from the *Physiologus*, often adding more animals and new interpretations. Much of the new material was influenced by or copied from three main sources. These were the *Etymologies* of Isidore of Seville, which looks at the origins of the names of creatures; Pliny's *Natural History*, which describes the habits and uses of many animals; and Solinus's *Collection of Memorable Things*, which is essentially a digest of Pliny's *Natural History*. The resulting expanded text provided the core material for the illustrated Latin bestiaries of the

12th and 13th centuries, and books such as these bestiaries would probably have been known to many of the Hereford map's medieval viewers. Others, without such privileged access to books, may still have heard of the existence of such creatures through stories and travellers' tales passed on by word of mouth, or through moral tales told in the sermons of the day. Moreover, they would almost certainly have seen images of beasts in the decorative carvings of parish churches, cathedrals and other significant buildings like monasteries.

Given the popularity of bestiaries, it is perhaps surprising that amongst the texts relating to animals on the Hereford map there is no direct reference to the Christian allegories spelled out in many of the bestiary manuscripts. A number of animals on the map are mentioned simply by name alone; the lion, for instance, and the crocodile, have no explanation or description. Others, like the unicorn and the rhinoceros, are given a longer text that refers specifically to Solinus or Isidore, but there is no written pointer to the lessons from the bestiaries. However, although there are no explicit textual references, there are similarities in some of the drawings. Amongst others, the drawings of the *manticore* and the *bonnacon* in particular share characteristics with pictures in bestiaries, as do the representations of the lynx and the elephant. So although the written texts do not appear to be influenced by morals taken from bestiaries, there is certainly a link between some of the pictures of animals on the map and a number of bestiary images. But it is unclear whether this is due to the map's artist copying from standard pattern books, or from another map, or from bestiary images themselves.

Whilst the map contains many exotic creatures, there is a peculiar lack of common domestic and farm animals. It seems strange that, on a map otherwise strewn with the beasts of the world, Europe is an almost animal-free zone. This is especially curious as the map was created at a time when animals were hugely important to the everyday life of all orders of society. Animals were essential for transport, haulage, travel, farming and hunting. Moreover animal products, too, were vital, not just for their pelts, their leather and their wool, but also for providing the materials of book manufacture and the spread of learning. It could be argued that on the map the European countries are so full of town and city icons that no room is left for animals. But perhaps there is also another reason. Perhaps the lack of explicit bestiary morality on the map, and the scarcity of familiar European work-a-day animals and domestic pets, is an indication that the primary reason for the inclusion of beasts was neither to moralise nor to represent the commonplace. Perhaps, instead, it was simply to show where in the world the curious and the exotic might be found. Whatever the principal reason for including these animals on the map, the popularity of bestiaries in the Middle Ages suggests that their moralities and sacred allegories were almost certainly known to the map's medieval audience.

The following list of beasts begins at the top of the *mappa mundi* with the dragons that are just below the earthly Paradise, and moves down the map towards the Pillars of Hercules at the bottom. Each animal is given its English name, followed by the map's Latin.

Dragons, *Dracones*

There are two pairs of dragons on the map. One pair, in the east, just below Paradise, are pictured flying upwards from the mountains of gold, their long necks entwined (Fig. 4.1). The other pair are shown frolicking over the triangular island of *Taprobane* (Sri Lanka), off the coast of India (Fig. 4.2). One of them,

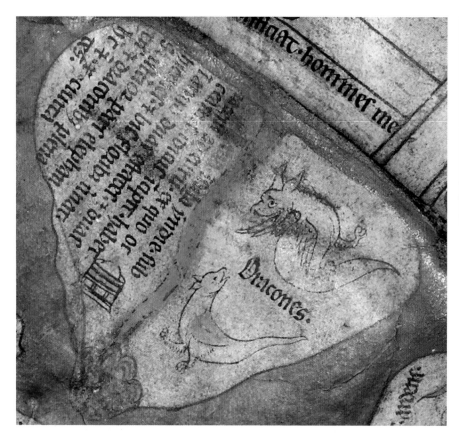

Fig. 4.1 (above)
The pair of dragons pictured
just below Paradise

Fig. 4.2 (left)
Taprobane (Sri Lanka)
and its pair of dragons

with its mouth open, seems to twist and turn in the air as it flies over a mountain on the southern tip of the island. Solinus speaks of a mountain surrounded by many dragons who beat the air with their wings, and Isidore of Seville tells how the Mountains of Gold in India are surrounded by dragons.[4] Perhaps these accounts explain the proximity of both the map's pairs of dragons to mountains.

The dragon was considered monstrous, dangerous and evil. Bestiaries describe it as the largest of all serpents, killing not by poison, but by twining its long coils around its prey or by the strength of its beating tail. Moreover, according to many bestiaries, dragons prey particularly on elephants. The message embodied in the characteristics of the dragon is an important one. In the words of the Aberdeen Bestiary:

> The Devil is like the dragon; he is the most monstrous serpent of all; he is often aroused from his cave and causes the air to shine because, emerging from the depths, he transforms himself into the angel of light and deceives the foolish with hopes of vainglory and worldly pleasure.[5]

Elephant, *Elephantes*
Near the coast of India is an elephant (Fig. 4.3). Weighted down by the castle he carries on his back, he droops his head towards the ground and his expression is one of forbearance. His body shape, ears, tusks

Fig. 4.3 The elephant and parrot

and tail are all very elephant-like, but his trunk ends in a peculiarly large circular swelling, and his mallet-shaped feet, too, are zoologically unrealistic. There are many medieval illustrations and carvings of elephants, with many variations in detail ranging from rounded bear-like ears to cloven hooves; it is unlikely that most artists had actually seen an elephant! The map's elephant, however, is amongst the most realistic of medieval representations.

Legends about elephants abounded in the Middle Ages. The text on the map tells us that India is home to enormous elephants with teeth believed to be made from ivory, and that the Indians put towers on elephants to use them in battle. But this brief account on the map makes no mention of the long descriptions of the habits of elephants or of the moralising that is included in many bestiaries. The *Aberdeen Bestiary*, for instance, details at length how elephants are monogamous and travel to the East, near Paradise, to mate. Here, the female seduces the male with the fruit of the mandrake. Two years later, the female gives birth in water because this will provide protection from the dragon, the enemy of the elephant. The explanation given by the *Aberdeen Bestiary* is that the elephants represent Adam and Eve, who were innocent until Eve tempted Adam with the fruit of the tree of knowledge. After the temptation, Eve conceived and gave birth on the waters of guilt. The same bestiary also relates a salvation story, in which a small elephant representing Christ saves a larger elephant from falling prey to a hunter.[6]

Parrot, *Spiticus*

The parrot perches on the side of a mountain in India, just to the left of the second 'I' of the gilded capitals spelling 'India' (Fig. 4.3). Its colours have faded, but its hooked bill is still just distinguishable. The text on the map says that Solinus tells us the parrot comes from India, is green, and has a purplish-red colouring around its neck. The map's text follows closely the words in the *Expositio Mappe Mundi*, although the *Expositio*, echoing Solinus more exactly, says that India 'alone' produces parrots.[7] Isidore of Seville tells us how parrots can be taught to imitate speech, and one bestiary explains that a parrot will learn best when it is young, but if it does not learn, then it should be hit over the head with an iron bar![8] The siting of the parrot on a mountain is perhaps a little curious. There is a parrot on a mountain in a couple of other medieval maps, but parrots in bestiaries are more often pictured on a leafy branch in a tree. However, this mountainous landscape can perhaps be seen to compare with the text of the *Expositio Mappe Mundi*, where the entries preceding and following the information about the parrot both refer to mountains in India.

Lizard, *Lacertus*

In the middle of Asia, scuttling northwards towards the sources of the Rivers *Acesines* and *Ydaspes*, is a picture of a large reptile with red ears (Fig. 4.4). Its four legs are splayed out, lizard-like, but its head is very similar to the axe-wielding dog-heads on the promontory in the Northern Ocean. It is labelled, simply, *Lacertus,* lizard.

Fig. 4.4 The lizard

Isidore of Seville includes lizards in his chapter on snakes and venomous creatures, and tells us that they are called *lacertus*, the Latin term for the upper arm, because they have 'arms'.[9] Some bestiaries, following Isidore, describe the lizard as a kind of reptile with limbs.

Alerion, *Alerion*

In the east, just below Paradise, is a pair of birds with large, slightly hooked bills (Fig. 4.5). They gaze at each other as they look backwards over their shoulders. The text tells us that these are the alerion birds, and that there is only one pair in the world. The birds are not mentioned by Isidore of Seville or Solinus, but they do appear in a French bestiary, the *Bestiaire* of Pierre de Beauvais, and they are also mentioned in versions of a fictitious letter, the Letter of Prester John, which told of fabulous creatures found in the East, and which circulated widely from the 12th century onwards.[10] The legend says that the alerion is like a large eagle with razor-sharp wings and that there is only one pair in the world. Some accounts say the alerion lives for 60 years, and others, 40. When their life span is over, the birds lay eggs that take 60 (or 40) days to incubate, and when the chicks hatch, the parents, accompanied by a flock of other birds, fly to the sea and dive to their death, leaving the other birds to care for their young.[11]

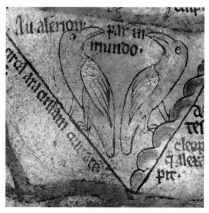

Fig. 4.5 The alerion

Pelican, *Pellicanus*

The representation of the pelican on a nest, bending her head downwards to draw blood from her chest to feed her young, is a common medieval image (Fig. 4.6). Known as 'the Pelican in her Piety', it came to be understood as emblematic of Christ's sacrifice for the sins of humanity, appearing in both art and heraldry. The legend of the pelican is quoted by many, including St Augustine, Isidore, and the bestiary compilers. There are a number of variations of the story, but the theme remains the same: one of the parent birds slays the young, and three days later revives them with their own blood.

The use of the first person in the succinct sentences on the map is interesting. The text reads: 'The pelican I am called. For my chick's sake

Fig. 4.6 The pelican

Fig. 4.7 The camel

I rend my heart.' Perhaps this first-person usage might be partially explained by Psalm 102, verse 6, which begins 'I am like a pelican of the wilderness'.

Camel, *Camelos*

Pictured on the opposite side of the *Memarnau* mountains from the pelican is a cheery-looking camel (Fig. 4.7). He is a Bactrian camel, with two humps. The text is from Solinus, and reads: 'Bactria has extremely strong camels that never wear their feet out'.[12] Pliny refers to Bactrian camels with two humps but, misleadingly, Solinus and Isidore both claim that the Arabian camel, not the Bactrian, has two humps. Some bestiaries, too, refer to a Bactrian camel with one hump, so it is interesting that the camel on the map, correctly, has two. In the bestiary tradition, camels signify the humility of Christ, who bears the sins of humanity.

Tiger, *Tigris*

The tiger is pictured walking away from a tree towards the Caspian Sea (Fig. 4.8). This is one of the very few trees on the map and is perhaps meant to signify the forested area of *Hyrcania* where Pliny, Solinus and Isidore all locate the tiger. In one of its more detailed texts, the map tells us that 'The tiger is a

beast; when it sees its cub captured, roused to action, it pursues the one fleeing with its cub, but this thief, taking flight with the gait of a swift horse, sets up a mirror in front of the tiger and so, unhindered, escapes.'[13] This information is characteristic of bestiary descriptions, where the tiger is often pictured looking into a mirror, distracted by its image, while the thief escapes. Ideas about reflected images and the ability of mirrors to pervert or distract from reality were often used as metaphors for immoral behaviour in sermons, homilies and moral treatises of the Middle Ages.[14]

Fig. 4.8 The tiger

Manticore, *Manticora*

The map tells us that '[According to] Solinus, the manticore is native to India, with a triple set of teeth, the face of a human, yellow eyes, the colour of blood, a lion's body, a scorpion's tale, a hissing voice'.[15] But the illustration on the map does not quite fit the description (Fig. 4.9). With a pointed chin that makes it look as though the map's manticore is possibly intended to be bearded, a spiky hair-do, and a fierce expression, he strides purposefully away from a tree. His face is certainly human, but there is no evidence of three rows of teeth, and the tail is not scorpion-like. There is an element of savagery about his determined ferocity, however, and bestiary lore also has it that the manticore eats human flesh. One bestiary illus-

Fig. 4.9 The manticore

tration, in MS Bodleian 764, shows a manticore carrying a half-eaten human leg in its mouth.[16]

Fig. 4.10 The marsok

Marsok, *Marsok*

To the south of Damascus there is a peculiar beast with a hairy back, a bushy tail and four strangely mismatched feet (Fig. 4.10). He has perky ears, a dog-like head, and a friendly, biddable expression. This is the map's *marsok*. We are told he is a miraculous 'transforming' creature. The picture on the map gives him one webbed foot, one cloven hoof, one paw and one human foot. The marsok doesn't appear in medieval bestiaries and seems to be peculiar to the Hereford map. However some bestiaries include a *parandrus*, a horned, ox-like beast mentioned by Pliny and Solinus, that can transform itself, and change colour if threatened. Bevan and Phillott suggest that the map's marsok might have a connection to the *parandrus*, but the resemblance is slight and the name very different.[17]

Phoenix, *Phenix*

The phoenix on the map looks rather like an eagle (Fig. 4.11). It stands facing northwards with its wings folded and its large talons clutching the top boulders of an unnamed mountain. But mountains do not usually feature in myths about the phoenix, so this drawing is perhaps not a reference to its story. Perhaps,

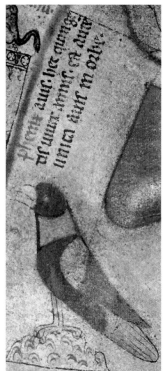

Fig. 4.11 The phoenix

instead, it should be seen in the same way as the rocky pedestals that many of the map's strange races stand on, that is, as a display platform for a curious or unique specimen, and a statement of its 'otherness'. The text on the map tells us that the phoenix lives 500 years and that there is only one of them in the world. There are many variations of the phoenix myth, but the main thread of the story remains the same; after 500 years the bird is consumed in incense-laden fire, and a new bird rises from the sweet-smelling ashes. The theme is one of rebirth, and the resurrection allegory is spelt out in many bestiaries, but there is no direct mention of this allegory on the map.

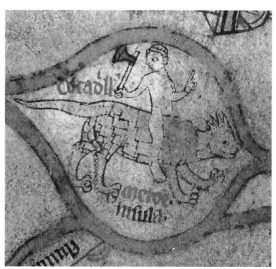

Fig. 4.12 The crocodile
(rotated 90° clockwise)

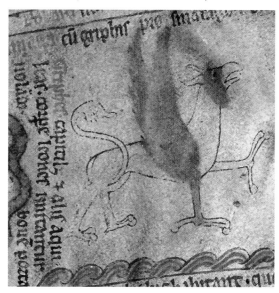

Fig. 4.13 The griffin

Crocodile, *Cocadrillus*

On the island of *Meroe* in the River Nile a naked man wielding an axe sits astride a four-legged, smiling, spiky-headed beast that is labelled *cocadrillus* (Fig. 4.12). Crocodiles of varying shapes and appearances feature in bestiaries, but the inclusion of a crocodile-rider in the picture is an unusual addition. Perhaps some light can be thrown on this, though, by Scott Westrem. He points out that the 12th-century monk Hugh of St Victor, in a written description of the geography and peoples of the world known as the *Descriptio Mappe Mundi*, describes how the people of *Meroe* are able to subdue and tame crocodiles.[18]

The allegory in a number of bestiaries teaches that crocodiles are like hypocrites who live a depraved life but none the less appear to be trustworthy, honourable and holy.

Griffin, *Griphes*

The map's griffin conforms to the bestiary norms of appearance; he has a lion's body, an eagle's head and wings (Fig. 4.13). He is placed towards the northern extremes of the land, and stands in a characteristically aggressive pose, with one talon raised as though he is about to attack. On the map he confronts the *Arimaspi* people, but bestiaries typically picture the griffin attacking a horse or an ox and describe him as living in Ethiopia or India.

Pines, *Pines*

Not far from the griffin, and framed by a triangular arrangement of mountain ranges, is the pines; a creature with a human face, a serpent's tail, two human feet and a ruffed collar (Fig. 4.14). Bevan and Phillot dismiss the pines as a creature for which they can 'give no account'.[19] However, Scott Westrem suggests that the title 'pines' might be a corruption of the word 'sphinx'. Many illustrations of the sphinx are in fact similar in attitude and body-shape to the pines on the map, which would seem to support Westrem's suggestion.

Tigolopes, *Tigolopes*

The tigolopes is yet another strange creature with an obscure origin. Sitting back on his haunches, the tigolopes gazes upwards at a pole topped by plant-like petals or leaves which he holds above his head (Fig. 4.15). He has large webbed feet and a tail, wears a coif (medieval headgear that looked something like a modern baby-bonnet), and seems to have a partial necklace of beads, or perhaps bells, around his neck. Bevan and Phillot have no suggestions about sources, but Scott Westrem cites the *Letter of Prester John* where tigolopes are listed amongst the strange races, but without a description.[20] Whether the tigolopes of the map should be classed as a beast or as one of a strange race of humanoids is a matter for discussion, but perhaps his tail and webbed feet put him more in the category of beast than strange human.

Fig. 4.14 The pines

Fig. 4.15 The tigolopes

Bonnacon, *Bonnacon*

This is a curly horned, bovine sort of a beast. The map tells us that: 'Native to Phrygia is an animal called bonnacon, with the head of a bull, mane of a horse, horns intricately twisted. With vehement voiding of its bowels, it sprays excrement the length of three acres, the heat of which is such that it scalds whatever it hits.'[21] The map's bonnacon is drawn walking in a northerly direction across the vellum looking backwards over his shoulder (Fig. 4.16). He has a slightly puzzled expression and his tail is raised as he evacuates his bowels. In some respects the picture perfectly illustrates the text's explicit description, but the bonnacon's surprised expression suggests that perhaps there is more to the story than appears on the map. A comparison of the map's bonnacon with a typical bestiary illustration can help supply the details. In a number of bestiaries the bonnacon looks backwards over his shoulder at hunters who are attacking him from behind with spears.[22] The drawing of the bonnacon on the map conforms to this standard pose, but although there are no hunters with spears on the map, the creature's perturbed expression can perhaps be explained by the story told in bestiary images.

Fig. 4.16 The defecating bonnacon

68

Fig. 4.17 The eale

Eale, *Eale*

Pictured directly beneath the phoenix is a hooved creature with a mane and what appears to be a slightly bemused expression. This is a yale or eale Fig. 4.17). He looks a little like a unicorn, but has two horns, one pointing forwards and one pointing back. Perhaps this ambivalence is the reason for his perplexity. The large block of text to the left of the eale explains his strange appearance in words directly ascribed to Solinus: the eale has the body of a horse, the tail of an elephant and the jaws of a goat, and is black in colour. With his flexible horns he can defend and attack at the same time.[23]

Sphinx, *Spinx*

The sphinx on the map is surrounded on all sides by mountains. Some are particularly peaked and jagged, and a line of text says that these are the highest mountains in Ethiopia (Fig. 4.18). This sphinx is not like other images of the sphinx. Instead of four legs and a lion-like body, she has only two legs and a writhing, serpentine tail. She does, however, have the wings and feminine face that are common to many carvings and drawings of the sphinx. The text on the map tells us that the sphinx has the wings of a bird, the feet of a serpent and the face of a girl.

Fig. 4.18 The sphinx

Lynx, *Linx*

The map's lynx is an evil-eyed, ferocious looking creature (Fig. 4.19). He bares his teeth and curls his upper lip as he paces towards the southern shore of the Black Sea looking back over his shoulder, his claws extended. The lynx's extraordinarily large eyes might be intended to signify his legendary keen eyesight and ability to see through walls. On the map the text says: 'The lynx sees through walls and urinates a black stone', and like a number of drawings of the lynx in bestiaries, the illustration shows a ball-shaped blob underneath his body. It hangs from a line that is, presumably, meant to be a stream of urine.[24]

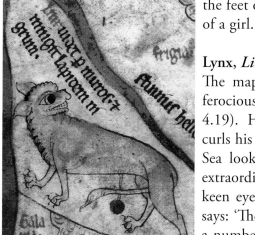

Fig. 4.19 The lynx

Cirenus Bird, *Avis Cirenus*

Another peculiarity of the map is the cirenus bird. To the south of Jerusalem, and near a circular feature that represents the well at Beersheeba, is a large parrot-type bird with a hooked bill and a hat-like crest on his head (Fig. 4.20). Its feet are more like paws than a bird's feet, and it looks backwards over its shoulder. The name *cirenus* is somewhat mysterious. Scott Westrem has no suggestion, but refers to Bevan and Phillot, who suggest that there might be a connection with the *cinnamolgus*. This was thought to be a cinnamon-eating bird. It appears in bestiaries and is cited by Pliny, Solinus and Isidore.[25] However bestiary images of the *cinnamologus* usually show a bird nesting high up in a tree; this is quite a different image from that on the map.

Fig. 4.20 The cirenus bird

Salamander, *Salamandra*

Just beneath the range of Joseph's 'store houses' is a drawing of a large, winged, lizard-like creature with a line of spots down its back (Fig. 4.21). It scuttles its winding way across the vellum with wings outstretched. Wings on a salamander are unusual; most bestiary illustrations of salamanders show creatures like snakes or lizards that

Fig. 4.21 The salamander

have no wings. All the same, the short reference on the map to the salamander's venom is in keeping with the bestiary tradition that claims the salamander is the most poisonous of all lizards. Many bestiaries, following the lead of Isidore of Seville, also speak of the salamander's legendary abilities to poison apples, infect water supplies and survive fire.[26]

Mandrake, *Mandragora*

Near the salamander, and on the bank of the Nile, is a mandrake (Fig. 4.22). It looks a little like an upside-down female figure with a strangely sculptured hairstyle and foliage sprouting from her upwardly pointing limbs. Although a plant, the mandrake often appears in bestiaries. The text on the map explains that the mandrake is a very miraculous plant, but doesn't say why. Bestiaries and herbals (books of plants), however, are more helpful. The mandrake root was thought to have many qualities and uses. It acted as an aphrodisiac for elephants and there was a long list of medicinal qualities that were useful for humans. These included curing headaches, earache, gout and epilepsy, and generally driving

Fig. 4.22 The mandrake

away infection. Unfortunately, gathering the mandrake root was problematic. The plant was said to scream as it was pulled from the ground, and this scream was believed to cause madness or death to those who heard it. Some accounts of mandrakes, though, suggest a solution to the problem: if a hungry dog is tied to the plant, and his food placed out of reach, the dog will rush forward for his food and pull the plant up. The dog's owner, of course, needs to be out of earshot! Some illustrations of the mandrake plant include a dog chained to its stem.[27]

Rhinoceros and Unicorn, *Rinosceros and Monoceros*

Across the Nile from the mandrake is a beast labelled rhinoceros, but his only truly rhinoceros-like feature is the horn on his nose. Beneath him stands a unicorn with an extremely long and candy-cane twisted horn coming from his forehead (Fig. 4.23). The map gives separate long blocks of text for each of

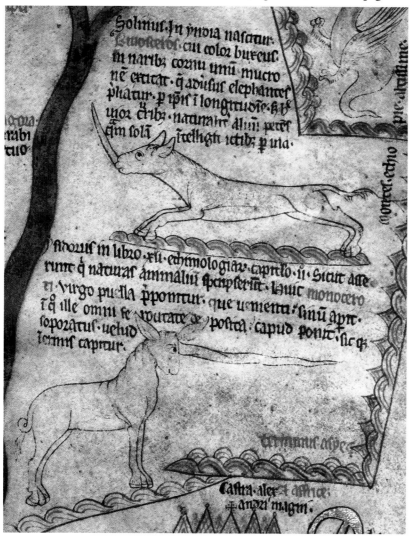

these creatures, but Isidore of Seville and many bestiaries call them both *monoceros*, having 'one horn', and conflate the descriptions of the two beasts as though they were one.

The map treats them differently. Naming Solinus as its source, it says that the rhinoceros shoots out a sharply pointed horn from its nose and fights with elephants, with which it is equal in length but shorter in limbs.[28] But although the rhinoceros is meant to fight with elephants, he is nowhere near the elephant on the map.

Referring to the unicorn, labelled *monoceros*, the map is also extremely explicit about its source. The description is one of the longest on the map, giving uncharacteristically detailed information about the source of its information and the legendary behaviour of the Monoceros. It reads: 'According to Isidore in book twelve chapter two of the Etymologies, as those who write about the nature of animals claim: a virgin girl is brought before this monoceros, and on his approach she bares her breast,

Fig. 4.23 The rhinoceros (top) and unicorn

71

on which he rests his head – all ferocity abandoned – so that, stupefied, he is captured like a harmless creature.'[29] In the medieval God-centred understanding of the natural world, the legendary behaviour of the unicorn is read as an allegory for the life of Christ, who became man and was made incarnate in a virgin's womb.

Ostrich, *Ostricius*

The map's ostrich is a tall bird with un-bird like cloven hooves and a small v-shaped tail (Fig. 4.24). It struts in a northerly direction, upstream, along the bank of a river that flows from a small range of mountains towards the Black Sea. In many bestiaries we are told that the ostrich eats iron, and it is pictured eating an iron horseshoe, but this is not the case with the picture on the map. We also learn from bestiaries that the ostrich lays an egg in the sand and then deserts it, leaving the warmth of the sun to hatch the chick. The ostrich pictured on the map appears to do neither of these things, but the text on the map, as well as describing the ostrich's goose-like head, body of a crane, and inability to fly, does refer to the ostrich eating iron.[30]

Fig. 4.24 The ostrich

Some bestiaries find a lesson in the ostrich's abandonment of its eggs, saying that man should learn from this to cast aside earthly things and trust in heaven. The *Aberdeen Bestiary*, though, likens the ostrich to hypocrites who:

> … pretend to live a life of piety, giving the impression of holiness without the reality of holy behaviour. They certainly have wings, as far as appearance goes, but in terms of action, they creep along the ground, because they spread their wings only to give an illusion of holiness.[31]

The Aegean She-Goat

An animal with a dog-like head, cloven hooves and a fat belly is pictured standing on the island of Lemnos in the Mediterranean Sea (Fig. 4.25). It carries a rectangular sign on its back that says *Egea*, The Aegean. Similar rectangular signs mark seas and other notable features that make up the Mediterranean, for example one is labelled *Helles pontus* (The Dardanelles), but the Aegean label is the only one carried by an animal. It is possible that this image is influenced by Isidore of Seville. In his *Etymologies*, Isidore tells us that:

Fig. 4.25 The Aegean she-goat

> Between Tenedos and Chios there is in the sea a rock – rather than an island – which is believed to look, to those who view it from a distance, like a she-goat, which the Greeks call 'aiga' – and from this the Aegean Sea is named.[32]

On the map, the creature is indeed placed between Tenedos and Chios (*Choos* or Kos), and although its head is not very goat-like, it certainly has cloven hooves. Perhaps, too, its swollen belly is intended as a sign of pregnancy. If so, it is definitely female!

Fig. 4.26 The mermaid

Mermaid

On the map a fish-tailed mermaid, pictured in the Mediterranean Sea, holds up a mirror (Fig. 4.26). She is not looking into it herself, instead she looks towards the right while seeming to hold the mirror to the viewer. Mermaids with a female body and fish tail have become part of today's cultural mythology, but in the Middle Ages ideas about mermaids were often fused with ideas about sirens. These were seductive bird-maiden or bird-men creatures; half bird and half human, sometimes with webbed feet, sometimes with talons, and often with wings. In legends, the exquisite singing of sirens or mermaids lured sailors to a certain death. One bestiary (MS Bodley 764) pictures three fish-tailed mermaids doing just this: the sailors have fallen into a charmed sleep, the sail is slack, and the three mermaids appear to have taken control of the boat. The text of the bestiary, however, describes them as sirens; 'deadly creatures, which from the head down to the navel are like men, but their lower parts down to their feet are like birds'.[33] Another manuscript, the *Queen Mary Psalter*, has a drawing at the bottom of a page of two sirens or mermaids with a ship. Both are female. One is fish-like and, like the mermaid on the map, is holding a mirror, while the other is bird-like. They too have enchanted a ship full of sailors, who have fallen asleep. On the following page is an illustration of both creatures attacking the sleeping sailors.[34]

The mermaid on the map takes almost centre stage in the Mediterranean, but there is no text relating to her. The only mention of mermaid-like creatures on the map is a short reference to many sirens on an island in the southern ocean, off the coast of Africa. But although there are many varied and conflicting descriptions and illustrations of mermaids and sirens from the Middle Ages, the moral warning for the medieval reader or viewer of the map remained the same: beware of the mermaid's mirror and do not be deceived or tempted by the easy pleasures and delights of this world.

Ape, *Simea*

In the north, near Norway, an ape strikes a very ape-like pose (Fig. 4.27). He sits with one leg extended and one leg bent at the knee. With his right arm he reaches across his front and around the left-hand side of his body to scratch beneath his armpit, while with his left hand he holds food, possibly fruit, to his opened mouth. The only text is the word *simea*. In his *Etymologies,* Isidore of Seville explains that

Fig. 4.27 The ape

this is a Greek word meaning 'pug-nosed', 'whence we name apes, because they have flattened nostrils and an ugly face, with disgustingly baggy wrinkles'. And he continues: 'Some people think that apes are named from a Latin word, because they are felt to have great similarity (*similitudo*) to human behaviour, but this etymology is false.'[35] Even so, a number of bestiaries claim that apes are so called because of their tendency to ape human behaviour, and some have illustrations of apes mimicking physicians, or wearing clothes and copying the behaviour of students and teachers in a school. Some bestiaries liken apes to the devil.

The map gives no explanation for why its ape is in Scandinavia.

Fig. 4.28 The bear

Bear, *Ursus*

In northern Europe, in what appears to be a land empty of towns and cities just beyond the area labelled 'upper Germany', there is an outline of a large bear (Fig. 4.28). Bestiaries claim that bear cubs are born shapeless and that they are 'licked into shape' by their parent, but this legend does not figure on the map. The text reads simply, '*ursus*', and the picture shows no hint of the bestiary legend.

The fish of the Mediterranean

As well as the mermaid there are a number of fish in the Mediterranean. Most are unnamed. One, a large rounded fish swimming towards Italy and away from the island of Crete, is upside down (Fig. 4.29). The others are all longer and thinner; more serpentine. One of these snake-like fish, swimming just beneath the upside-down fish, seems to have a mouthful of teeth and a line of spots down its body (Fig. 4.29). Only one fish is named. This is the 'sea-soldier', a large fish swimming along the coast of Italy with a sword strapped to its side (Fig. 4.29).[36] The *Aberdeen Bestiary* holds up the behaviour of fish as a model for humanity, saying that male fish know nothing of adul-

Fig. 4.29 Fish

Fig. 4.30 The basilisk

Fig. 4.31 The scorpion

Fig. 4.32 The lion

tery, and that female fish protect their young as if in a 'fortress', swallowing them live and then bringing them back 'whole'.[37]

Basilisk, *Basiliscus*

In medieval mythology the basilisk was a small, highly venomous spotted snake, with a crested head or the head of a cockerel. Isidore tell us that the word *basilisk* is 'a Greek word translated into Latin as 'little king' (*regulus*), because it is 'the king of the snakes'.[38] Some bestiaries also refer to the basilisk as a cockatrice, although some accounts treat the basilisk, the regulus and the cockatrice as three separate creatures. The map's basilisk has a coiled serpent's tail, a bird's head and the hooked beak of a cockerel, but no cockscomb on his head (Fig. 4.30). However, the artist has drawn a small circular feature hanging underneath the creature's head and beak. Perhaps this was intended to be a cockerel wattle. Although it was a mere six inches long, the basilisk was considered the most evil of all snakes. Its smell alone could kill, and it could slay a man with its evil glance. The bestiary manuscript Bodley 764 says that the basilisk 'signifies the devil, who openly kills the heedless sinner with his venom'.[39]

Scorpion, *Scorpio*

One of the oddest beasts on the map in terms of both its appearance and location is the scorpion that is drawn near the River Main, east of the River Rhine (Fig. 4.31). With a crab-like body, no head and no legs, the drawing seems to be unfinished. The creature does, however, have two pincers and a long, thin, upwardly curving tail with a roundish feature at its tip that is possibly intended as a stinger. Bestiaries usually depict the scorpion as a lizard or worm-like creature found in the desert. Scott Westrem mentions the slim possibility that this picture might refer to the Scorpio of the Zodiac.[40]

Lion, *Leo*

The map's lion is drawn in Africa near an oval-shaped lake at the western extreme of a river named the Nile (Fig. 4.32). He walks away from the course of the river with his head held high, proudly, and his tail curled over his back in a heraldic s-shape. The text on the map says, simply, 'Lion', but various bestiaries read detailed Christian allegories into the behaviour of lions. The following is taken from the *Aberdeen Bestiary*:

Those who study nature say that the lion has three main characteristics. The first is that it loves to roam amid mountain peaks. If it happens that the lion is pursued by hunters, it picks up their scent and obliterates the traces behind it with its tail. As a result, they cannot track it. Thus our Saviour, a spiritual lion, of the tribe of Judah, the root of Jesse, the son of David, concealed the traces of his love in heaven until, sent by his father, he descended into the womb of the Virgin Mary and redeemed mankind, which was lost.

Not knowing of his divine nature, the Devil, the enemy of mankind, dared to tempt him like an ordinary man. Even the angels on high did not know of his divinity and said to those who were with him when he ascended to his father: 'Who is this king of glory?'

The second characteristic of the lion is that when it sleeps, it seems to have its eyes open. Thus our Lord, falling asleep in death, physically, on the cross, was buried, yet his divine nature remained awake; as it says in the Song of Songs: 'I sleep but my heart waketh'; and in the psalm: 'Behold, he that keepeth Israel shall neither slumber nor sleep'.

The third characteristic of the lion is that when a lioness gives birth to her cubs, she produces them dead and watches over them for three days, until their father comes on the third day and breathes into their faces and restores them to life. Thus the Almighty Father awakened our Lord Jesus Christ from the dead on the third day; as Jacob says: 'He will fall asleep as a lion, and as a lion's whelp he will be revived'.[41]

The lion is marked by a single word on the map, but it is an image that would very probably have had multiple meanings and mystical significance for the map's medieval audience.

Leopard, *Leopard*

Across the mountains from the lion is a leopard, and as with the lion, the only text is his name, 'leopard' (Fig. 4.33). Scott Westrem points out that the leopard's raised front paw and his tail held over his back in an s-shape, render him almost a mirror image of the lion. Interestingly, Isidore of Seville, in his *Etymologies,* has a theory about a connection with the etymology of the name, saying that the leopard is the product of an adulterous mating between a lion and a panther (*pard*). Perhaps, in the light of this etymological theory, the visual connection with the lion on the map is intentional. The leopard embodies the reflected, but not the true image of the lion.

Fig. 4.33 The leopard

Ants, *Formice*

Positioned just above the description of the one-eyed king of the Agriophagi in Africa are two ants (Fig. 4.34). They stand facing each other, keeping guard over a row of small dots. Each of them appears to have a long proboscis-type projection from the head. The text has elements in common with a number of sources, but Scott Westrem suggests that the wording possibly derives more directly from Hugh of St Victor.[42] It reads 'Here enormous ants hoard golden sands'. This is a reference to a legend about ants the

76

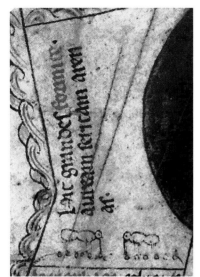

Fig. 4.34 The ants

size of dogs which appears in typical bestiary accounts of ants. However, in many bestiaries the treatment of ants goes far beyond mere description and legend. It has a moral aspect about wise and prudent living, and a mystical significance to do with understanding the word of the Bible. Men should learn from the habits of ants. Like ants they should industriously collect 'grain' and lay in stores for the future. Moreover, they should pay attention to the habit of ants in selecting wheat instead of barley, as an indication from God that they should choose true Christian teachings and reject heretical dogma. The bestiary in MS Bodley 764 has this to say:

> The third habit of the ant is this: at harvest time it wanders through the cornfields, and tests the blades with its mouth, to see if they are barley or wheat. If it is barley it goes to another blade and smells it, and if it finds that it is wheat, it climbs up the stalk, takes the corn and carries it home … Hence Job's saying: 'Barley grew for me instead of wheat' [31:40], that is, the teachings of heretics, for these are only barley and you should keep them far from you, because they corrupt men's souls and destroy them. Oh Christian flee from all heretics, whose teachings are false and enemies of the truth.[43]

Bull, *Buglossa*

In southern France there is a sketch of a bull. It is one of very few animals in the European quarter of the map (Fig. 4.35). There is no further explanation, and its name is something of a mystery. Bevan and Phillot observe that *buglossa* is the Latin name for the plant 'ox-tongue', and not an animal at all. They suggest that the misnomer could be either intentional word-play, or simply a mistake. Scott Westrem, following a different train of thought, points out that the drawing of the bull might potentially be a reference to the 'Taurus' of the zodiac but he concedes that this is, nevertheless, unlikely, because there is not a consistent attempt to represent the zodiac on the map.

Fig. 4.35 The bull

Genet, *Geneis*

In the Iberian peninsula is a drawing of a long-tailed four-footed animal with a pointed face. The map calls this a genet (Fig. 4.36). Genets are not commonly illustrated in bestiaries, and the reason for the inclusion of the genet on the map is something of a mystery considering the general lack of animals in Europe, but genet fur was traded in the Middle Ages, and common genets are found in south-western Europe.

Fig. 4.36 The genet

These, then, are the beasts that lurk in the spaces of the map. Many of the texts are short, but for the map's medieval viewers the names and images of these beasts would have brought to mind associations rooted in the bestiary morals and popular legends of their own time.

5   LAST WORDS

There is much more that could be said about the Hereford *Mappa Mundi*. This book does not pretend to have included mention of all the texts and images on the map. But before concluding, there is one more important scene that should not be missed.

At the bottom of the map, on the right-hand side, a horseman on a finely decorated stallion rides away from the rim of the world, raising his hand as he looks back, while a forester with two dogs stands behind him, and the words *passe avant* ('go ahead', or 'pass beyond') hang in the space between them (Fig. 5.1). There have been a number of interpretations of this scene. Meryl Jancey sees the rider as coexistent with the map's viewers, and about to travel the world. He looks back, she says, 'with a wave of his

Fig. 5.1 The rider in the bottom right-hand corner of the map

79

hand to the great round world above his head'.[1] Brian Levy, in his very wide-ranging research, points to resonances with stories of Alexander the Great and his horse Bucephalus, as well as the four horsemen of the apocalypse, various chivalric heroes from *chansons de gestes*, and Christ as the rider of the white horse in Revelation 19: 11. But he sees the rider as simply waving to the huntsman behind him.[2] Naomi Reed Kline understands the scene as representing the transitory nature of the medieval present, which must pass, and she also describes the rider as bidding goodbye.[3] Valerie Flint has a different approach, based on the politics of the late 1270s. Her suggestion is that the rider represents Thomas Cantilupe, Bishop of Hereford 1275-1282, celebrating winning a legal case against the Earl of Gloucester over the right to hunt on the Malvern Hills, and raising his hand in acknowledgement to the huntsman who allows him to pass.[4] But as Paul Harvey has pointed out, more recent scholarship dates the map considerably later than Cantilupe's political struggles, and casts doubt over Flint's interpretation.

Many interpretations have been suggested but the scene remains enigmatic. The horse is elaborately decorated. Festooned with bells and ornamental shields, and with a crupper bearing an orb surmounted by a cross, this is clearly a stallion intended for a significant purpose. As the horse walks away from the rim of the world, the rider turns. His right hand is raised to his eyes and he looks backwards at the world he is leaving. This gesture is usually interpreted as a wave, but perhaps there is a different interpretation. Perhaps instead of a wave, the rider's hand is raised in a symbolic gesture; a gesture that draws attention to his eyes and perhaps denotes 'sight' or 'vision'. The meaning of 'gesture' in art works of the medieval West is a topic well researched by art historians, and perhaps applying knowledge from this field of study might help lead to a better understanding of the Hereford map's rider and his huntsman. Research in this area is ongoing, but until more is understood, the rider must remain enigmatic.[5]

There is much still to learn about this fascinating map and its history. Despite extensive research, the purpose of the map and where it hung in the cathedral remains a subject of conjecture; there is, after all, no absolute evidence of its existence in Hereford Cathedral before Thomas Dingley saw it there in 1684. Moreover its images and texts almost certainly still have secrets to yield. But some things are best pondered over in the imagination, and I like to think that long ago, in a small city on the far western border of England, people clustered curiously around this cloth of the world, pointing to Ethiopian marvels and strange Indian beasts. And in their mind's eye they were transported through time and space to ancient and Biblical times, or to the far-flung and exotic temples, citadels and wonders of the medieval world.

Bibliography

Printed Sources

Augustine, *Confessions*. A New Translation by Henry Chadwick (Oxford University Press, 1991)

Augustine, *Concerning the City of God, against the Pagans*. Translated by Henry Bettenson with a new introduction by G.R. Evans (Penguin Classics, 2003)

Bailey, Martin. 'The Discovery of the Lost Mappamundi Panel: Hereford's map in a Medieval Altarpiece?' In *The Hereford World Map: Medieval World Maps and Their Context*, ed by P.D.A. Harvey (British Library, 2006) pp.79-94

Barber, Richard. *Bestiary: Being An English Version of the Bodleian Library, Oxford M.S. Bodley 764 translated and introduced by Richard Barber*. Paperback edition (Boydell Press, 1999)

Bede, *The Reckoning of Time*. Translated with introduction, notes and commentary by Faith Wallis, (Liverpool University Press, 1999)

Bestul, Thomas H. 'Walter Hilton' in *Approaching Medieval English Mystical and Anchorite Texts*, ed by Dee Dyas, Valerie Edden and Roger Ellis (D.S. Brewer, 2005)

Bevan, W.L. and Phillot, H.W. *Medieval Geography: An Essay in Illustration of the Hereford Mappa Mundi* .(E. Stanford, 1873)

Clarkson, Christopher. 'The Hereford Map: The First Annual Condition Report' in *The Hereford World Map: Medieval World Maps and Their Context*, ed by P.D.A. Harvey (The British Library, 2006), pp.95-106.

Crone, G.R. 'New Light on the Hereford Map' in *The Geographical Journal*, 131.4 (December 1965) pp.447-462.

Dingley, Thomas. *History from Marble Compiled in the Reign of Charles II by Thomas Dingley; gent*. Facsimile ed. John Gough Nichols (Camden Society, 1867)

Flint, V.J. 'The Hereford Map: Its Author, Two Scenes and a Border' in *Transactions of the Royal Historical Society*, 6th series, 8 (1998) pp.20-44

Friedman, John Block. *The Monstrous Races in Medieval Art and Thought*. (Syracuse University Press, 2000)

Gautier Dalché, Patrick, ed. *La Descriptio Mappe Mundi de Hugues de Saint-Victor*. (Etudes Augustiniennes, 1988)

Gautier Dalché, Patrick. 'Décrire le monde et situer les lieux au XIIe siècle: L'*Expositio mappa mundi* et la généalogie de la mappemonde de Hereford' in *Mélanges de l'École Française de Rome. Antiquité-Moyen Âge*, 112. 1 (2001) pp.343-409

Dilke, O.A.W. 'Maps in the Service of the State: Roman Cartography to the End of the Augustan Era' in *The History of Cartography*, Vol.1, ed by J.B. Harley and David Woodward, pp.201-211

Dilke, O.A.W. *Greek and Roman Maps*. (John Hopkins University Press, 1998)

Harvey, P.D.A., *Mappa Mundi: The Hereford World Map*. 3rd edn (Hereford Cathedral, 2010)

Isidore of Seville, *Etymologies*. Translated with an introduction and notes by Stephen A. Barney, W.J. Lewis, J.A. Beach and Oliver Bergof (Cambridge University Press, 2011)

Jancey, Meryl. *Mappa Mundi. The Map of the World in Hereford Cathedral*. (Dean and Chapter of Hereford Cathedral, 1987, 94 and 95).

Jones, Richard. *The Medieval Natural World*. (Pearson Education Ltd., 2013)

Kline, Naomi Reed. *Maps of Medieval Thought: the Hereford Paradigm*. (Boydell Press, 2001)

Levy, Brian J. 'Signes et communications 'extraterrestres'. Les inscriptions marginales de la mappemonde de Hereford' in *Das Grosse Abenteuer der Entdeckung der Welt im Mittelater* or *La grande aventure de la découvert du monde au moyen âge*, ed. Danielle Buschinger and Wolgang Spiewok. Greifswalder Beiträge zum Mittelater/Études Médiévales de Greifswald 43 [WODEN Ser.56]. Jahrbücher der Reineke-Gesellschaft/Annales de la Société Reineke Ser.4[6]. (Greifswald: Reineke, 1995) pp.35-48

Morgan, Nigel. 'The Hereford Map: Art-Historical Aspects' in *The Hereford World Map: Medieval World Maps and their Context*, ed. P.D.A. Harvey (British Library, 2006) pp.119-135

Parkes, Malcolm, 'The Hereford Map: The Handwriting and Copying of Text' in *The Hereford World Map: Medieval World Maps and their Context*, ed. P.D.A. Harvey (British Library, 2006) pp.107-117

Paulus Orosius, *The Seven Books of History Against the Pagans*. Trans. by Roy J. Deferrari (Catholic University of America, 1964)

Peter of Limoges. *The Moral Treatise on the Eye*. Trans. by Richard Newhauser (Pontifical Institute of Medieval Studies, 2012)

Pseudo-Methodius. *Apocalypse & An Alexandrian World Chonicle*. Ed and trans. by Benjamin Garstad (Harvard University Press, 2012)

Solinus, Caius Julius. *The Excellent and Pleasant Worke: Collectanea Rerum Memorabilium of Caius Julius Solinus*. Trans. 1587 by Arthur Golding. A Facsimile Reproduction, with an Introduction by George Kish (Scholars' Facsimiles and Reprints, 1955)

Terkla, Daniel. 'The Original Placement of the Hereford *Mappa Mundi*' in *Imago Mundi* 2004, Vol.56, Part 2, pp.131-151

Thomson, Rodney. 'Medieval Maps at Merton College Oxford' in *Imago Mundi* 2009, Vol.61, Part 1, pp.84-90

Tyers, Ian. *Tree-ring Analysis of the Hereford Mappa Mundi, project 782A*. (University of Sheffield Arcus Dendrochronology Laboratory, 2004)

Wesselow, Thomas de. 'Locating the Hereford *Mappamundi*' in *Imago Mundi* 2013, Vol.65, Part 2, pp.180-206

Westrem, Scott D. *The Hereford Map: A Transcription and Translation of the Legends with Commentary*. (Brepols, 2001)

Voragine, Joacobus de. *The Golden Legend*. Selected and translated by Christopher Stace (Penguin, 1998)

Electronic Sources

Aberdeen Bestiary, Aberdeen University Library, Univ. Lib. MS 24. http://www.abdn.ac.uk/bestiary/translat/66r.hti. Last accessed 6/03/2015

British Library, Harley MS 1585. http://www.bl.uk/manuscripts/FullDisplay.aspx?ref=Harley_MS_1585. Last accessed 06/03/2015

British Library, Royal MS 2 B VII. http://www.bl.uk/manuscripts/Viewer.aspx?ref=royal_ms_2_b_vii_f084r. Last accessed 06/03/2015

Dante's Letter to Cangrande Della Scala. English translation. Georgetown University. http://faculty.georgetown.edu/jod/cangrande.english.html. Last accessed 06/03/2015

Harley, J.B. & David Woodward (eds). *The History of Cartography*. http://www.geography.wisc.edu/histcart/. Last accessed 06/03/2015

Layamon, *Brut*. Project Gurenberg Ebook. http://www.gutenberg.org/ebooks/14305. Last accessed 06/03/2015

Medieval Bestiary. http://bestiary.ca/beasts/beastgallery80.htm. Last accessed 06/03/2015

MS Ashmole 1511. http://bodley30.bodley.ox.ac.uk:8180/luna/servlet/view/search?q=Shelfmark=%22MS.%20Ashmole%201511%22. Last accessed 06/03/2015

Pegolotti's Merchant Handbook. English translation. Washington University. http://depts.washington.edu/silkroad/texts/pegol.html. Last accessed 06/03/2015

Pliny, *Natural History*. Perseus Digital Library. http://www.perseus.tufts.edu/hopper/text?doc=Plin.+Mat.+toc. Last accessed 06/03/2015

The Letter of Alexander to Aristotle, BL MS Cotton Vitellius A XV trans. by Andy Orchard, http://members.shaw.ca/sylviaolk/Beowulf2.htm. Last accessed 06/03/2015

The Travels of Sir John Mandeville. Project Gutenberg Ebook.http://www.gutenberg.org/files/782/782-h/782-h.htm. Last accessed 06/03/2015

References

Chapter 1 A Curiosity in the Library

1. Thomas Dingley, *History from Marble,* facsimile ed. by John Gough Nichols (London: Camden Society, 1867) p.clx. Dingley's original work was compiled in the 1680s. Despite Dingley's confidence that the map was made by a monk, scholars today think that this is doubtful.

2. The word 'vellum' derives from French, *vélin,* referring to a calf, whilst the word 'parchment' can refer to any, unspecified skin. Today the words 'vellum' and 'parchment' are sometimes used interchangeably.

3. Christopher Clarkson, 'The Hereford map: the first annual condition report', *The Hereford World Map: Medieval World Maps and their Context*, ed by P.D.A. Harvey (London: The British Library, 2006), p.100.

4. M.B. Parkes, 'The Hereford Map: the handwriting and copying of the text', *The Hereford World Map: Medieval World Maps and Their Context,* ed by P.D.A. Harvey (London: British Library, 2006), pp.107-117. Hereafter, Parkes.

5. Nigel Morgan, 'The Hereford Map: art-historical aspects', *The Hereford World Map: Medieval World Maps and Their Context,* ed by P.D.A. Harvey (London: British Library, 2006), p.100.

6. Parkes, p.110.

7. For a comprehensive account of the map's sources see Scott D. Westrem, *The Hereford Map* (Turnhout: Brepols, 2001), pp.xxvii-xxxviii. Hereafter, Westrem, *Hereford Map.*

8. Patrick Gautier Dalché, 'Décrire le monde et Situer les lieux au XII siècle', *Melanges de L'Ecole Francais de Rome, Moyen Age* 113/1 (2001), (with the *Expositio Mappe Mundi*) pp. 343-409. Hereafter, Gautier Dalché, *Décrire le monde* and *Expositio Mappa Mundi.*

9. W.L. Bevan and H.W. Phillot, *Mediaeval Geography; an Essay in Illustration of the Hereford Mappa Mundi,* (E. Stanford: London, 1873), p.23. Hereafter, Bevan and Phillot.

10. Sarah Arrowsmith, *Vision and Mystical Ecstasy: Some Thoughts on the Spirituality of the Hereford Map.* unpublished paper given at the Leeds International Medieval Congress, 2013.

11. I Corinthians, 13:12.

12. Peter of Limoges, *The Moral Treatise on the Eye,* trans. by Richard Newhauser (Toronto: Pontifical Institute of Medieval Studies, 2012), pp.12-13.

13. Marcia Kupfer has recently completed research on this topic, which is, as yet, unpublished. Her findings will be of great interest.

14. The term 'prebend' refers to a portion of the cathedral's estates, the profits of which would have provided an income.

15. See Valerie Flint, 'The Hereford Map: Its Author(s), Two Scenes and a Border', *Transactions of the Royal Historical Society*, 6th Series. 8 (1998), pp.19-44.

16. Westrem, *Hereford Map,* p.xxiii.

17. Gautier Dalché, *Décrire le monde* and *Expositio Mappe Mundi,* pp.348-351.

18. P.D.A. Harvey, *Mappa Mundi: The Hereford World Map* 2nd edn (Hereford: Hereford Cathedral, 2010), p.18. Hereafter, Harvey, *Mappa Mundi.*

19. 'The Discovery of the Lost Mappamundi Panel', *The Hereford World Map: Medieval World Maps and their Context*, ed by P.D.A. Harvey (London: The British Library, 2006), p.79. The back panel had been discarded in 1948 and the map re-housed in a new case.

20. Ian Tyers, *Tree-ring Analysis of the Hereford Mappa Mundi*, project 782A, University of Sheffield Arcus Dendrochronology Laboratory, 2004, p.7.

21. Bede, *The Reckoning of Time,* translated with introduction, notes and commentary by Faith Wallis, (Liverpool: Liverpool University Press, 1999), p.91.

22. There is evidence that the 11th-century monk Hugh of St Victor used a *mappa mundi* as a teaching aid. See *La Descriptio Mappe Mundi de Hugues de Saint-Victor*, ed. by Patrick Gautier Dalché, (Paris: Etudes Augustiniennes, 1988). Additionally, Rodney Thompson has discovered references to a *mappa mundi* used for lectures in the library at Merton College Cambridge. See Rodney Thompson, 'Medieval Maps at Merton College', Oxford, *Imago Mundi* 2009, Vol. 61, Part 1: 84-90.

23. See Dan Terkla, 'The Original Placement of the Hereford *Mappa Mundi*', *Imago Mundi* 2004, Vol.56, Part 2: 131-151, and Thomas de Wesselow, 'Locating the Hereford *Mappamundi*', *Imago Mundi* 2013, Vol.65, Part 2: 180-206.

Chapter 2 From Eden to Doomsday

1. For a literate medieval audience, the seated Emperor come Pope figure might have suggested a reference to the Donation of Constantine. This was a forged document by which Constantine the Great was supposed to have transferred supremacy over the Western Roman Empire to the Pope. The document was proved a forgery in the 15th century, but at the time the Hereford map was made, it is likely that the Donation of Constantine was thought by many to be genuine.

2. Trans. by Westrem, *The Hereford Map*, p.9.

3. Medieval accounts of the survey commissioned by Julius Caesar report not three surveyors, but four. See O.A.W. Dilke, 'Maps in the Service of the State: Roman Cartography to the End of the Augustan Era', *The History of Cartography,* Vol.1, ed by J.B. Harley and David Woodward, p.205. http://www.press.uchicago.edu/books/HOC/HOC_V1/HOC_VOLUME1_chapter12.pdf last accessed 15/12/2014.

4. O.A.W. Dilke, *Greek and Roman Maps* (Baltimore and London: John Hopkins University Press, 1998), p.40.

5. Trans. by Westrem, *The Hereford Map*, p.11.

6. Trans. by Westrem, *The Hereford Map*, p.107.

7. Further down the river Euphrates another tower has been drawn. The label next to it reads *terra babilonie,* 'Land of Babylonia'. Scholars are divided about which drawing is intended as Babylon and which as the Tower of Babel, but as the largest structure is so vast and straddles the River Euphrates, just as Ancient Babylon is described as doing, it seems to make most sense to read this larger construction as Babylon, with the Tower of Babel reaching upwards from its topmost storey.

8. See Thomas H. Bestul, 'Walter Hilton', *Approaching Medieval English Mystical and Anchorite Texts,* ed by Dee Dyas, Valerie Edden and Roger Ellis (Cambridge: D.S. Brewer, 2005), p.92. Also http://d.lib.rochester.edu/teams/text/bestul-hilton-scale-of-perfection last accessed 18/12/2014.

9. The Travels of Sir John Mandeville is a fictitious travelogue that appeared in the middle of the 14th century. See http://www. gutenberg.org/files/782/782-h/782-h.htm especially Chapter VII. Last accessed 02/01/2015.

10. The medieval map known as the Sawley map, Corpus Christi College Cambridge MS 66 *c.*1190, has a picture of granaries very similar to that on the Hereford map.

11. The Latin Vulgate Bible, attributed to St Jerome in the 4th century AD, translated and brought together earlier versions of the Bible. By the time of the Hereford *Mappa Mundi* it was the text in common use.

12. Trans. by Westrem, *The Hereford Map*, p. 93.

13. Trans. by Westrem, *The Hereford Map*, p.125.

14. Layamon, Brut, l. 5079. See also http://www.gutenberg. org/ebooks/14305 last accessed 02/01/2015.

15. Trans. by Westrem, *The Hereford Map*, p.165.

16. See Westrem, *The Hereford Map,* p.116 and p.118.

17. http://faculty.georgetown.edu/jod/cangrande.english.html last accessed 17/12/2014.

18. http://www.newadvent.org/cathen/11590b.html last accessed 17/12/2014.

19. The Golden Legend, *Legenda Aurea,* is a book telling the lives of the saints. The original manuscript is thought to have been compiled by Jocobus de Voragine in the mid 13th century. In its time the book was very popular and many hundreds of manuscripts still exist today. When printing was introduced to England in the 15th century, it was one of the first books to be printed by William Caxton.

20. Augustine, *Confessions*, A New Translation by Henry Chadwick (New York: Oxford University Press, 1991), p.3.

21. Joacobus de Voragine, *The Golden Legend*, selected and translated by Christopher Stace, (London: Penguin, 1998), pp.113-115.

22. Trans. by Westrem, *The Hereford Map*, p.409.

23. Isidore of Seville, *Etymologies.* Translated with an introduction and notes by Stephen A. Barney, W.J. Lewis, J.A. Beach and Oliver Bergof (Cambridge: Cambridge University Press, 2011), XV, ii, 36, p.307. Hereafter, Isidore, *Etymologies.*

24. Westrem, *The Hereford Map*, p.102.

25. Westrem*, The Hereford Map*, p.214.

26. See Westrem, *The Hereford Map*, p.398.

27. Westrem, *The Hereford Map*, p.324.

28. In Shakespeare's *Julius Caesar*, Cassius, speaking of Caesar, says, 'Why, man, he doth bestride the narrow world Like a Colossus, and we petty men Walk under his huge legs and peep about To find ourselves dishonourable graves.' Act 1 Sc. 2 ll 136-139.

29. Westrem, *The Hereford Map*, p.427.

30. Trans. by Westrem, *The Hereford Map,* p.71.

31. Trans. by Westrem, *The Hereford Map*, p.137.

32. Pseudo-Methodius, *Apocalypse*, ed and trans. by Benjamin Garstad (Cambridge Massachasettes and London: Harvard University Press, 2012), p.131.

33. See R.K. Morris, 'The Architectural History of the Medieval Cathedral Church', in *Hereford Cathedral, A History* ed by

Gerald Aylmer and John Tiller (London: Hambledon Press, 2000), pp.218-220.

34. Parkes, pp.111-112.

35. Parkes, pp.111-112.

36. See Westrem, *Hereford Map*, p.322.

37. See Paulus Orosius, *The Seven Books of History Against the Pagans* trans. by Roy J. Deferrari (Washington: Catholic University of America, 1964), pp.xv-xx.

38. See http://www.newadvent.org/cathen/08279b.html.

39. G.R. Crone, 'New Light on the Hereford Map', *The Geographical Journal* Vol 131 Part 4, December 1965, p.452.

40. *ibid.*

41. http://depts.washington.edu/silkroad/texts/pegol.htmml.

42. G.R. Crone, 'New Light on the Hereford Map', *op.cit.*, p.452.

Chapter 3 A Tall Tale

1. *The Excellent and Pleasant Worke: Collectanea Rerum Memorabilium of Caius Julius Solinus*, Translated 1587, by Arthur Golding. A Facsimile Reproduction, with an Introduction by George Kish. (Scholars' Facsimiles and Reprints, 1955).

2. *Saint Augustine, Concerning the City of God, against the Pagans*, translated by Henry Bettenson with a new introduction by G.R. Evans, (London: Penguin Classics, 2003) p.664.

3. *The Letter of Alexander to Aristotle*, BL MS Cotton Vitellius A XV ff 107-131, trans. by Andy Orchard, http://members.shaw.ca/sylviavolk/Beowulff2.html last accessed 7/02/2014.

4. The Psalter World Map is British Library Add. MS. 28681, fol. 9r. The Ebstorf map was destroyed in an air raid over Hanover in 1943. The original was made on 30 goatskins and was about 12 feet in diameter. Fortunately it had been photographed in 1891 and various drawings have been based on this photograph. The Duchy of Cornwall fragment is housed at the Duchy of Cornwall office in London.

5. Bodleian MS Douce 88. This manuscript collection contains 2 separate bestiaries, ff. 5r-33v and ff. 68r-114r. It is the second of these that begins with a treatise about monstrous races.

6. Westrem, *Hereford Map*, p.49.

7. Westrem, *Hereford Map*, p.57.

8. Isidore, *Etymologies*, XI.iii.7, p.244; also Westrem, *Hereford Map*, p.33.

9. Book of Enoch, VII; 2. The Book of Enoch is a Jewish text that is not included in the Old Testament. Medieval theologians had access to a number of religious texts that most Christian churches do not regard as canonical today.

10. Gautier Dalché, *Decrire le monde* and *Expositio Mappa Mundi*, p.357.

11. John Block Friedman, *The Monstrous Races in Medieval Art and Thought* (New York: Syracuse University Press, 2000), p.136. Hereafter, Friedman, *Monstrous Races*.

12. Isidore, *Etymologies*, XI.iii.21, p.245.

13. Westrem, *Hereford Map*, p.375.

14. Isidore, *Etymologies*, XI.iii.24, p.245. Westrem, *Hereford Map*, p.374.

15. Westrem, *Hereford Map*, p.135.

16. Friedman, *Monstrous Races*, p.124.

17. Friedman, *Monstrous Races*, p.25.

18. Isidore, *Etymologies*, XI.iii.11, p.244.

19. Friedman, *Monstrous Races*, p.16.

20. Westrem, *Hereford Map*, p.381.

21. Gaius Julius Solinus, *The Excellent and Pleasant work of Julius Solinus Polyhistor*. Translated out of Latin into English, by Arthur Golding. Gent., London: Thomas Hacket, 1587. Chapter XXXIX, f. Siii r.

22. Quoted in Friedman, *Monstrous Races*, p.128.

23. Friedman, *Monstrous Races*, p.15.

24. Westrem, *Hereford Map*, p.357

25. Westrem, *Hereford Map*, p.346.

26. Friedman, *Monstrous Races*, p.124.

27. Friedman, *Monstrous Races*, p.124.

28. Westrem, *Hereford Map*, p.137.

29. Westrem, *Hereford Map*, p.100.

30. Dalché, *Decrire le monde* and *Expositio Mappe Mundi*, p.354.

31. Westrem, *Hereford Map*, p.95.

32. Westrem, *Hereford Map*, p.98.

33. Westrem, *Hereford Map*, p.99.

34. Friedman, *Monstrous Races*, p.126.

35. Dalché, *Decrire le monde* and *Expositio Mappe Mundi*, pp.380-382.

Chapter 4 Myth and Reality

1. See Richard Jones, *The Medieval Natural World* (Harlow: Pearson Education Ltd., 2013), p.76.

2. The manuscript of the Old English verse Physiologus is contained in a manuscript at Exeter Cathedral known as 'The Exeter Book' or 'Codex Exoniensis', Exeter Dean and Chapter MS 3501.

3. The Old English Physiologus, Text and Prose translation by Albert Stanborrough Cook. http://www.gutenberg.org/files/14529/14529-h/14529-h.htm, last accessed 2/01/2015.

4. Isidore of Seville, *Etymologies*. Translated with an introduction and notes by Stephen A. Barney, W.J. Lewis, J.A. Beach and Oliver Bergof (Cambridge: Cambridge University Press, 2011), XIV.iii.7, p.286. Hereafter, Isidore, *Etymologies*.

5. Aberdeen Bestiary, Aberdeen University Library, Univ. Lib. MS 24, f 66r. http://www.abdn.ac.uk/bestiary/translat/66r.hti, last accessed 27/10/2014.

6. *ibid*.

7. Gajutier Dalché, *Décrire le monde* and *Expositio Mappa Mundi*, p.75.

8. Isidore, *Etymologies*, XII.vii.1, p.263; and *Bestiary MS Bodley 764*, translated by Richard Barber (Woodbridge: Boydell Press, 2010), p.129. Hereafter, Barber, *Bestiary*.

9. Isidore, *Etymologies*, XII.iv.34, p.257.

10. Prester John was a fabled ruler of a mythical Christian kingdom somewhere in the exotic East. The 'Letter of Prester John' told of strange marvels of the East. Scholars believe that he and his letter were almost certainly fictitious.

11. See Westrem, *Hereford Map*, p.54.

12. Trans. by Westrem, *Hereford Map*, p.77.

13. *ibid.*, p.75.

14. See Richard Newhauser's introduction to Peter of Limoges, *The Moral treatise on the Eye* (Toronto: Pontifical Institute of Medieval Studies, 2012), pp.xii-xxiv.

15. Trans. by Westrem, *Hereford Map*, p.77.

16. Barber, *Bestiary*, p.63.

17. Pliny, *Natural History*, Bk8 chapter 52. http://www.perseus.tufts.edu/hopper/text?doc=Perseus:text:1999.02.0137:book=8:chapter=8:chapter=52&highlight=tarandrus, last accessed 6/08/2014.

18. Westrem, *Hereford Map*, p.130

19. Bevan and Phillot, p.67.

20. Westrem, *Hereford Map*, p.108.

21. Trans. by Westrem, *Hereford Map*, p.235.

22. Barber, *Bestiary*, p.47; also MS Ashmole 1511, f.18r, http://bodley30.bodley.ox.ac.uk:8180/luna/servlet/view/search?q=S helfmark=%22MS.%20Ashmole%201511%22, last accessed 02/01/2015; also http://bestiary.ca/beasts/beastgallery80.htm, last accessed 13/8/2014.

23. Westrem, *Hereford Map*, p.122,

24. Trans. by Westrem, *Hereford Map*, p.143.

25. Bevan and Phillot, p.80

26. Isidore, *Etymologies*, XII. iv.35, p.257.

27. British Library, Harley MS 1585, fol. 57r; http://bestiary.ca/beasts/beast1098.htm, last accessed 02/01/2015.

28. Trans. by Westrem, *Hereford Map*, p.133.

29. Trans. by Westrem, *Hereford Map*, p.433.

30. Westrem, *The Hereford Map*, p.188.

31. http://www.abdn.ac.uk/bestiary/translat/41v.hti, last accesssed 12/8/2014.

32. Isidore, *Etymologies*, XIII. xvi.5, p.278.

33. Barber, *Bestiary*, p.150.

34. British Library Royal MS 2 B VII. ff 96v-97r. http://www.bl.uk/manuscripts/Viewer.aspx?ref=royal_ms_2_b_vii_f084r, last accessed 14/8/2014.

35. Isidore, *Etymologies*, XII.ii.30, p.253.

36. Westrem, *Hereford Map,* p.406, suggests this might be a mnemonic.

37. http://www.abdn.ac.uk/bestiary/translat/74r.hti, last accessed 15/8/2014.

38. Isidore, *Etymologies*, XII.iv.6-8, p.255.

39. Barber, *Bestiary,* p. 185

40. Westrem, *Hereford Map,* p. 228.

41. Aberdeen Bestiary, f.7r-7v, http://www.abdn.ac.uk/bestiary/translat/7v.hti, last accessed 15/8/2014.

42. Westrem, *Hereford Map*, p.306.

43. Barber, *Bestiary*, p.115. MS. Bodley 764, f.53v.

Chapter 5 Last Words

1. Meryl Jancey. *Mappa Mundi. The Map of the World in Hereford Cathedral* (Hereford: Dean and Chapter of Hereford Cathedral, 1987, 94 and 95), p.4.

2. Brian J. Levy, 'Signes et communications 'extraterrestres'. Les inscriptions marginales de la mappemonde de Hereford', in *Das Grosse Abenteuer der Entdeckung der Welt im Mittelalter* or *La grande aventure de la découvert du monde au moyen âge,* ed. Danielle Buschinger and Wolgang Spiewok. Greifswalder Beiträge zum Mittelater/Études Médiévales de Greifswald 43 [WODEN Ser.56]. Jahrbücher der Reineke-Gesellschaft/ Annales de la Société Reineke Ser.4[6]. (Greifswald: Reineke, 1995), p.40.

3. Naomi Reed Kline, *Maps of Medieval Thought: the Hereford Paradigm* (Woodbridge: Boydell Press, 2001), p.63.

4. V.J. Flint, 'The Hereford Map: Its Author(s), Two Scenes and a Border', *Transactions of the Royal Historical Society*, 6th series, 8 (1998), p.38.

5. Sarah Arrowsmith *Vision and Mystical Ecstasy: Some Thoughts on the Spirituality of the Hereford Map.* unpublished paper given at the Leeds International Medieval Congress, 2013; also see Jean Claud Schmitt, *La raison de Gestes dans l'Occident medieval* (Bibliothèque des Histoires, Gallimard, 1990).

Index